Edgar Cayce on

Auras & Colors

Also by Carol Ann Liaros

Intuition Made Easy

Also by Kevin J. Todeschi

Non-Fiction

Dream Images and Symbols: A Dictionary
Edgar Cayce's ESP
Edgar Cayce on the Akashic Records
Edgar Cayce on Reincarnation and Family Karma
Edgar Cayce on Mastering Your Soul Growth
Edgar Cayce on Soul Mates
Edgar Cayce's Twelve Lessons in Personal Spirituality
Edgar Cayce on Vibrations
God in Real Life
Soul Signs: Life Seals, Aura Charts, and the Revelation

Fiction

A Persian Tale
The Reincarnation of Clara
The Rest of the Noah Story

Edgar Cayce on

Auras & Colors

Learn to Understand Color and See Auras

Including the well-known Auras *booklet written by Edgar Cayce*

Kevin J. Todeschi & Carol Ann Liaros

A.R.E. Press • Virginia Beach • Virginia

6th Printing, July 2016

Printed in the U.S.A.

A.R.E. Press
215 67th Street
Virginia Beach, VA 23451-2061

ISBN 13: 978-0-87604-612-8

Cover design by Christine Fulcher

Auras are twofold. That which indicates the physical emanations, and that which indicates the spiritual development . . .

The aura, then, is the emanation that arises from the very vibratory influences of an individual entity, mentally, spiritually—especially of the spiritual forces.

Edgar Cayce reading 319-2

Table of Contents

Preface .... *ix*

Chapter One: Edgar Cayce on Auras and Colors 1

Chapter Two: The Vibration of Color 15

Chapter Three: The Meaning of Colors (Red, Orange, and Yellow) 27

Chapter Four: The Meaning of Colors (Green, Blue, Indigo, and Violet) 41

Chapter Five: The Meaning of Colors (White, Black, Gold, and All the Rest) 55

Chapter Six: Feeling Versus Seeing the Aura 71

Chapter Seven: Experiencing the Aura for Yourself 85

Conclusion 101

Appendix I: Auras: An Essay on the Meaning of Colors—*the only booklet written by Edgar Cayce (ca. 1944)* 107

Appendix II: Examples of Edgar Cayce's Waking Aura Descriptions 125

Appendix III: Color Dictionary—the Possible Meaning of Colors 131

References and Recommended Reading 141

About the Authors 143

Preface

In simplest terms the aura is a field of energy that emanates from all things. Some may see it as a band of color or colors; others might describe the appearance of an aura as waves of light or motion, and still others indicate that they can "feel" certain things just by being close to another person's energy. Those who can see or feel this band of energy or vibration insist that the aura provides descriptive information about the person, plant, living thing, or object from which the aura is emanating. Although the existence of this kind of energy might sound unusual to some people, what may be even more surprising is the fact that everyone can be taught to see or experience an aura.

In Western religious history the aura has been associated with the halo. In mysticism the aura is connected to the astral or non-physical body. Although some individuals contend that there is no such thing as an aura, in the twentieth century Kirlian photography provided what for many became scientific evidence for the existence of the aura. Kirlian photography is able to capture evidence of the energy fields surrounding all living things and can also depict phantom energy that is no longer present from a living object. For example, even after a leaf has been torn from a plant, a Kirlian photograph will still display a faint image of the leaf that has been removed.

Those who can see the human aura contend that it is the sum total of the individual—physically, mentally, emotionally, and spiritually. It can provide details about a person's health, life experiences, relationships, attitudes, strengths, weaknesses, moods, problems, thoughts, ideas, and even past lives. In the same way a fingerprint is unique to the individual the aura is unique, as well. Ultimately, the aura is the vibrational manifestation of everything that exists about a person.

Countless people have actually had experiences with the human aura without really knowing it at the time or realizing what they have encountered. Have you ever come in contact with another person and instantly had the feeling of wanting to take a step back, as though something was repelling you? Conversely, have you ever met someone for the very first time and had the feeling of being instantly drawn to that individual? Both of these experiences note how it can "feel" to be in proximity to another person's energy field or vibration. There is an instantaneous effect that another individual's aura and vibration have upon your own.

One of the early proponents of the existence of the human aura was Edgar Cayce (1877–1945), the most documented psychic of all time. Called the "father of holistic medicine" and "the sleeping prophet," Edgar Cayce became known for his incredible clairvoyant accuracy and for a psychic legacy that continues to help and inspire individuals around the world. For forty-three years of his adult life, Cayce possessed the ability to lie down on a couch, close his eyes, fold his hands over his stomach, and put his mind into an altered state in which virtually any type of information was available to him. The accuracy of Cayce's psychic work is evidenced by approximately one dozen biographies and literally hundreds of titles that explore the thousands of topics he discussed and various aspects of his information, as well as a thriving organization and a university that continue to exist based on his work. (Additional information can be found in *There Is a River* by Thomas Sugrue, *Edgar Cayce—A Seer Out of Season* by Harmon Bro, and *Edgar Cayce: An American Prophet* by Sidney Kirkpatrick, or by visiting www.EdgarCayce.org and www.AtlanticUniv.edu.)

When asked about the source of his information, Cayce replied that there were essentially two. The first was the subconscious mind of the individual for whom he was giving the reading and the second was the Akashic records. In further describing these records, Cayce stated: "Upon time and space is written the thoughts, the deeds, the activities of an entity . . . " (1650-1)[1] The Akashic records somehow maintain an account of everything that has transpired in the universe. Similarly, the human aura is the sum total of everything that has transpired in an individual's unique soul history, including the past times and the previous lives of that person. When asked to describe his personal experiences with auras, Cayce had this to say:

> Ever since I can remember I have seen colors in connection with people. I do not remember a time when the human beings I encountered did not register on my retina with blues and greens and reds gently pouring from their heads and shoulders. It was a long time before I realized that other people did not see these colors; it was a long time before I heard the word "aura," and learned to apply it to this phenomenon which to me was commonplace. I do not ever think of people except in connection with their auras; I see them change in my friends and loved ones as time goes by—sickness, dejection, love, fulfillment—these are all reflected in the aura, and for me the aura is the weathervane of the soul. It shows which way the winds of destiny are blowing. (See *Auras* booklet, Appendix I)

[1]The Edgar Cayce readings are numbered to maintain confidentiality. The first set of numbers (e.g., "1650") refers to the individual or group for whom the reading was given. The second set of numbers (e.g., "1") refers to the number of the reading for that individual or group.

Cayce gained a wealth of personal experience with the meaning of colors and energy patterns that he saw emanating from all individuals. He perceived the aura as a series of vibrating colors that surrounded an individual and provided a barometer of a person's health, state of mind, strengths, weaknesses, desires, thoughts, and more. In fact, Cayce believed that every thought and action possessed an energetic vibration that was essentially reflected in a person's aura.

In addition to perceiving the colors in auras throughout the many years he gave life readings to people—those readings which discussed the soul's history through time as well as personal strengths and weaknesses—Cayce frequently discussed which colors most aligned with an individual and which colors were most in tune with an individual's personal vibration. As a case in point, during a reading given to a nineteen-year-old stenographer who was apparently strong-willed, strong-minded, temperamental, and prone to condemning herself and others, Cayce advised her against ever wearing red, as the energy and vibration of the color would reinforce her negative attributes. Instead she was encouraged to wear delicate shades of grays and greens, as these colors would be more conducive to her temperament and more apt to inspire confidence in herself and others. (2522-1) Conversely, Cayce once advised a withdrawn, introverted, and subdued forty-four-year-old clerk that she needed to wear red in order to energize her own vibrations and give herself more "flash or show." He went on to say: " . . . For the vibrations of . . . {self} have even been so subdued about the entity that little of the real beauty has escaped, because the love and deep emotion had been kept hid so long." (3564-2)

Edgar Cayce repeatedly emphasized that color was a vibration and that each individual had an affinity to certain colors more than others because of her or his own level of soul growth and personal vibration. By utilizing the vibrations of certain colors, an individual could empower traits or abilities he or she needed to work on, whereas other colors might help to restrain or diminish undesirable characteristics.

One discussion of the use of vibrations occurred in a reading given to a thirty-seven-year-old woman who apparently needed more balance in her life. Her positive qualities included having a good sense of humor, possessing a great capacity for love, and often being perceived as someone who was extremely "sweet." On the other hand, the same woman was told that she was entirely too sensitive, which often adversely affected her relationships with others. Extremely hard-headed, she also exhibited a bad temper. In order to help in her daily interactions with others, the reading recommended the use of all seven principal colors at different times—red, orange, yellow, green, blue, indigo, violet—as well as black and white. The reading advised: " . . . For color itself is vibration, just as much vibration as—or even more than—music." (3637-1) By alternating the various colors, in time she would be able to achieve the balance she apparently needed. Cayce added, "By the colors indicated, ye can control almost thine own physical being, by thine own mind!"

Throughout his life Edgar Cayce gave additional readings that explored the importance of color. He gave readings on life seals, which discussed the creation of a unique personal symbol for motivation and inspiration, and aura charts, which contained a visual depiction of the soul's history through time. Cayce also gave readings on color symbolism such as that contained in dreams and in the Book of Revelation and discussed how certain past-life experiences could influence individuals to be more drawn to specific colors. There are literally hundreds of Cayce readings on the subjects of auras, colors, and personal symbolism.

In addition to Edgar Cayce, reputable contemporary psychics are also able to access the Akashic records as a source of information and can discuss how those records manifest in the lives of individuals. Many have also worked a considerable amount with auras. For example, according to psychic Carol Ann Liaros who has given readings for many decades: "An individual's aura is a personal manifestation of his or her Akashic records. Whatever is going on in the person's life is evident in the aura. An individual's aura changes as the body's physical health or vitality changes." When she sees gray spots around the heart area, for example, she knows that the individual has had a heart attack or has some other problem with the heart. Much like a networked computer system, from the aura it is possible to access anything contained within the central record itself.

Carol Ann began her psychic work back in the 1960s but was extremely surprised that life events led her in that direction. Her career began after friends convinced her to see a reputable psychic who gave Carol Ann a reading of her own. The individual told her that she was extremely psychic and that she would be using her intuition to teach others. He went on to say that Carol Ann would be doing extensive travelling with her teaching, that she would be working with "men in white coats, like doctors and scientists," and that she would write a book about her psychic experiences.

After the reading Carol Ann was convinced that the psychic had been wrong and that she had no intuitive talents of her own. However, her friends insisted that she try to give them readings. In time Carol Ann came to understand that not only she had intuitive talents, but everyone else did also. Eventually she told Hugh Lynn Cayce, Edgar Cayce's eldest son, about some of her psychic experiences; and he referred her to Dr. Justa Smith, a biochemist, educator, and nun, who was working with the Human Dimensions Institute at Rosary Hill College doing research with healers. Carol Ann's research with "the men in white coats" began.

Over the years Carol Ann Liaros has logged more than one million air miles in traveling to teach individuals how to use their own intuitive gifts. She eventually authored *Intuition Made Easy*, a book that explores how people can use and experience their psychic perception. When asked to describe her first experience seeing the human aura, Carol Ann recalls:

> I remember telling Dr. Justa Smith that seeing auras was not one of the intuitive skills I possessed. She asked me: "Don't you see colors or anything around people?" I told her I didn't. Sometimes I saw hazes and glows around people or behind people but I couldn't see auras and colors and discern when someone had a physical problem.
>
> Dr. Smith said, "Let's try an experiment. Take a look around me. Do you see anything around me?"
>
> Thinking that auras were in color and that I was only seeing a glow around her head, shoulders, and arms, I laughingly told her I couldn't see her aura. She persisted in questioning me. I looked at this grayish glow and said,

"There seems to be a break in it from about the bottom of your ear to your shoulder."

She said, "That's very interesting because I have a neck and shoulder problem that I'm being treated for and that's exactly where it is."

Well, being the skeptical, logical thinker that I am, I decided it had to be a coincidence. Besides, I could see the same kind of haze around tables, chairs, lamps, animals, and trees. I saw it around everything. My misconception at the time was that auras only radiated from human beings.

Soon afterwards, I began experimenting with this haze or glow. I might ask someone, "Do you have anything wrong with your ear?" because I might have seen a break there, not as much energy, or it looked aggravated. And they'd respond, "Yes, as a matter of fact, I have an earache." Persisting as the very logical person that I am, I went to the eye doctor and had my eyes checked. My eyes were fine.

Many, many months later when I finally began to see colors around people, I thought, "Oh, I have glaucoma. That must be what this is. It has nothing to do with seeing auras." And so again I went to the eye doctor. I did not have glaucoma, and I was still seeing colors around people.

One of Carol Ann's most fascinating experiences teaching individuals to see the human aura occurred while she was working with a class at the YWCA in Batavia, New York. She explained to the students what the aura was and how to begin seeing it by refocusing the eyes on a higher, finer level of energy. She then stood up against a white screen wearing her black outfit (so their minds wouldn't say, "that's only a reflection of the color") and had them do a relaxation exercise with their eyes closed. When they opened their eyes, they were asked to describe whatever they could see. Many saw a huge glow; others could see colors behind her, and so forth. One of the students in the class seemed to demonstrate a tremendous level of accuracy.

Carol Ann had several more students come up one at a time and stand with their backs against the screen in order to give the class the ability to see how one person's aura might look different from someone else's. Some saw different shapes, intensities, and colors; and again the same individual showed a real talent for seeing the human aura.

Finally Carol Ann asked for any volunteers to come forward who possessed a physical problem that wasn't obvious and couldn't be seen. These auras gave the students in the class the opportunity to see how the aura looked "different" wherever a physical issue was present—for example: wider, narrower, darker, lighter, bulging, or indented. The same male student proved to be talented with this exercise as he was able to see various shades of color and was able to pinpoint areas where there was a physical problem because the area "looked darker" to him.

After the class, the wife of the talented student came up and asked, "Did you see how well my husband did?" Carol Ann replied that he had done a great job. The wife added, "But, you don't know the best part—*my husband is totally blind!*"

Carol Ann was stunned. It turned out that the man was forty-one years old and had been blind since the age of fourteen, with no light perception. His wife had dragged him to the class because she didn't want to attend alone. He had also attended as a "non-believer." When he was asked how he had been able to see the auras, he thought for a moment and said, "Well, I did with my mind what you told the others to do with their eyes, and I could see it!" When he was asked to show where in his mind he had seen the auras, he pointed to the middle of his forehead—the third eye. This experience became the original impetus behind Carol Ann's founding and directing "Project Blind Awareness," which for many years was an innovative training program designed to enhance intuition in blind participants in order to help them become more mobile and independent. Presently, Carol Ann is convinced that anyone can be taught to experience the aura:

> Our eyes are accustomed to seeing on a very dense level of energy—this physical level. We appear to be solid but in reality our physical bodies are made up of millions of moving molecules with a lot of space in between the moving molecules. All it really takes to see an aura is an eye adjustment. We need to train ourselves to see on this higher,

finer level of energy. It is simply a conscious refocusing of the eye.

The purpose of exploring the aura is actually to better understand the self. In the same manner that tools such as astrology, psychic readings, numerology, psychological tests, personal introspection, dreams, and more can empower an individual to become all that she or he was meant to be, working with the aura can be beneficial in overcoming one's issues and in cultivating personal strengths. Most often the aura is ever changing, multi-layered, and multi-colored. The size, shape, and colors generally change and evolve depending upon what an individual is doing, what she or he is thinking and feeling, and whom or what the person is encountering. Like a mirror, the aura provides a reflection of the individual, but it is a reflection that details both the exterior and interior parts of one's self. The key to seeing auras is similar to undertaking the rest of the psychic processes. The key is being able to relax.

This book was written in order to provide individuals with information about the human aura—what it is and how it can be experienced. In addition to citing contemporary examples as well as examples from the life's work of Edgar Cayce, the book explores the meaning of colors and how the vibration of color can impact individuals. It also examines what colors may mean (positively and negatively) in the human aura. Even if you've never seen an aura before, or believed it was possible to see an aura, this book will give you the tools to experience the human aura. It is hoped that this book might make some small contribution to understanding the fact that each of us is much more than a physical body and that some of the tools we need in order to know the self have been with us all along—we just didn't know where to look.

Kevin J. Todeschi
Carol Ann Liaros

1 Edgar Cayce on Auras and Colors

The Edgar Cayce material examined in many ways not only the subject of color but also the idea of auras. A major area of exploration in the Cayce readings is that of personal symbolism. This topic is discussed in readings dealing with dreams and dream interpretation as well as the interpretation of personal signs and symbols (such as those contained in artistic renderings of what the readings referred to as life seals and aura charts). There was also a thorough exploration of symbolism undertaken by a group of individuals who called themselves the Glad Helpers Prayer Group. Although the primary interest of this prayer group was working with prayer, meditation, and spiritual healing, the group also obtained readings on a number of subjects that explored personal symbolism including the interpretation of the Book of Revelation and an exploration of the connection between the spiritual chakras and the endocrine glands of the physical body.

In terms of how personal symbolism was connected to the subjects of color, consciousness, and the body's physiology, the readings stated that as energy rose through the endocrine centers of the body there were symbols and colors associated with each of these centers, which could come to consciousness. For example, in the Book of Ezekiel in the Old Testament, the prophet Ezekiel while in prayer has a vision in which he sees four beasts caught up in a whirlwind: a man, a lion, an ox, and an eagle (Ezekiel 1:10). Similar imagery is witnessed five hundred years later by the Apostle John during his Revelation experience when he sees a lion, a man, a calf, and an eagle (Revelation 4:7). According to Cayce the images of these four beasts are actually associated with the four lower spiritual centers and can come to consciousness during meditation or prayer as the energy of the kundalini rises through the body. The symbolism association witnessed by both Ezekiel and John is as follows: the root chakra stands for a calf or an ox, the second chakra for a man or a human, the third chakra for a lion, and the fourth chakra for an eagle.

There are colors associated with each of the seven major chakras, which Cayce correlated to the body's seven major glandular (endocrine) centers. Each of these colors has its own vibration and is also associated with the raising of personal consciousness. Cayce told the group: " . . . For as has been given, color is but vibration . . . " (281-29) The higher the center, the higher the level of vibration and consciousness, so that the first chakra and its corresponding color are lower than the seventh chakra and its corresponding color. The colors of these chakras or glands are easy to remember since they occur in the same order as the colors of the rainbow—red, orange, yellow, green, blue, indigo, and violet:

Center / Chakra	**Endocrine Gland**[2]	**Associated Color**
1	Gonads	Red
2	Cells of Leydig	Orange
3	Adrenals	Yellow
4	Thymus	Green
5	Thyroid	Blue
6	Pineal	Indigo
7	Pituitary	Violet

[2]For a detailed discussion of the endocrine glands and the physiology of meditation, see *Meditation and the Mind of Man* by Herbert B. Puryear, PhD and Mark A. Thurston, PhD (Virginia Beach, VA: A.R.E. Press, 1983).

Although each of the colors corresponds to a level of consciousness and an understanding of what that color symbolized, Cayce also told the prayer group that personal associations and experiences with colors could supersede their generally accepted meaning. For example, while many individuals associate blue with spirituality and one's spiritual path, to some that color might be associated with depression and the experience of "feeling blue."

To be sure, an interest in color and an exploration of what colors may mean are not simply relegated to the Edgar Cayce information. Quite the contrary, for in the world of our perception color is all around us. Whether it is the vibrant greens of spring, the brilliant colors of summer, the orange and reds of autumn, or the intense white of our surroundings after a snowfall, color has always been a part of our environment. Throughout our lives, our relationship with color has an ongoing impact upon the clothes we wear, the cars we drive, the furniture we choose, and even the food that we choose to eat. Color is everywhere. But in a very real sense color is a collectively perceived illusion. What we think we see is actually a by-product of the way in which the vibration of visible light is perceived by the eyes and the brain.

In terms of the science of color, it has been proven that the yellow banana we ate for lunch does not actually exude the color yellow. Instead the banana absorbs all frequencies of visible light that are shining on it with the exception of those frequencies that are reflected and perceived as yellow. We perceive things as being specific colors because all objects absorb certain wavelengths and reflect others. The reflected wavelengths are those that reach the eye. We perceive color because of our ability to distinguish among these different wavelengths. The shortest wavelength (and highest frequency) that is generally visible to humans is violet, and the longest wavelength (and shortest frequency) that is generally visible is red. A wavelength is measured in an infinitely small measurement equating to a thousand millionth of a meter called a nanometer (nm), and the visible range is approximately 380 nm to 740 nm.

Although some might believe that white is the absence of color whereas black contains all colors, the reverse is actually true. It was Isaac Newton who discovered that white light divides into its color components when passed through a prism. He labeled those colors red, orange, yellow, green, blue, indigo, and violet. Often the science of color does not distinguish a difference between indigo and violet, therefore "visible light" is often associated with just six bands of color. [It is important to note that "visible light" in the animal kingdom is much different than that perceived by human eyes. For example, many birds see a wider range of colors than humans, including colors in the ultraviolet spectrum (light with a shorter nm wavelength than violet); conversely, dogs and cats are generally labeled as "color blind" because they see very pale colors or various shades of gray.] However, since both Newton and Cayce discussed the importance of these seven colors, they will certainly be worth examining later.

Two of the tools dealing with personal symbolism and colors that are distinct to the Edgar Cayce readings are life seals and aura charts.[3] Essentially, both of these tools are visual drawings and artistic depictions of symbols, images, and colors that Cayce suggested could assist each individual in better understanding him or herself. Life seals are drawings that individuals create, usually within a circle, that can help them better understand themselves. Similar to the use of mandalas by Carl Jung, these drawings contain colors, pictures, and images that have a symbolic importance to the individual. Ultimately, these seals serve as reminders of a person's talents as well as those things that the individual may need to work on in the present. Cayce once told a twenty-year-old woman that she had the ability to create life seals for others, and he described the purpose of these drawings:

> . . . that which will arouse in the inner self of individuals, individual minds, individual souls, that which will aid those individuals in knowing themselves, their weaknesses, their faults, their uprisings, their downsittings. That which enables the individual soul to see itself better. And that which aids each individual or hinders it, or is helpful to it in giving expression of itself in the present experience. 275-36

[3]For a detailed exploration of life seals and aura charts, see *Soul Signs* by Kevin J. Todeschi (Virginia Beach, VA: A.R.E. Press, 2003).

Building upon this use of personal symbolism as a means of understanding the self while also incorporating the concepts of reincarnation and soul memory, Edgar Cayce recommended the creation of what he called an aura chart. The aura chart is essentially a visual illustration of the soul's journey with pictures, images, colors, and symbols that portray what the soul has learned as well as where it has succeeded or failed in its passage through time and history. The aura chart depicts those lifetimes or incarnations that most influence the individual in the present—in other words those periods in history to which the individual feels most drawn and has the greatest emotional response (good or bad). Essentially, the aura chart is a visual representation of what Cayce referred to as the soul's Akashic record—the universal record or database of each individual's personal soul journey.

The first individual to request an aura chart reading was Cayce's secretary, Gladys Davis, who was told that a reading requesting " . . . the symbols, colors, and the meaning of each . . . " could be made into a drawing that would be helpful to her. (288-50) Later, a thirty-one-year-old auto salesman requested an aura chart for himself and was told of its purpose:

> In giving an aura chart—this we would indicate as to the high points in the experiences of the entity in the earth, having to do with the manner in which the entity has conducted or is conducting itself in the present for the greater unfoldment,—spiritually, mentally and materially . . .
>
> The beauty of such a drawing depends much upon the concept of the artist. Yet these may visualize for the entity that as may bring helpful influences into the experience.
>
> 533-20

The idea of using symbolism to facilitate personal growth and an expanding consciousness as well as a means of understanding one's inner self is connected to what transpires during the Jungian concept of individuation. Essentially, the process of individuation is one in which the conscious mind comes to terms with its inner Self, integrates the substance of the unconscious, and gradually moves toward personal wholeness. The disconnected nature of the human creature on its journey toward wholeness is often depicted in archetypal imagery, symbolism, dreams, visions, fairy tales, and myths. For example, although children's classics such as *The Wizard of Oz* and *The Adventures of Pinocchio* might be read as nothing more than entertaining stories, both are actually symbolic of the soul's journey toward personal wholeness and enlightenment.

As previously stated, Edgar Cayce's primary source of information while he was giving readings was the Akashic records. Cayce also discussed the connection between the Akashic records and the human aura, suggesting that the aura was in some ways a holographic image of the record itself, containing the very same type of information for the individual. For example, while giving a reading to a thirty-year-old oil prospector, Cayce discussed what he was seeing in terms of the individual's record:

> Yes, we have the body, the conditions here, and the record as has been made, and as will be made, both in the present and past and future, as we see from conditions existing in the present sphere or aura of the individual. All is not good, yet in many phases of earth's sphere, known as success, this individual will rise high, yet ever those of the wandering forces . . . 221-2

And while beginning a physical reading regarding the health of a thirty-four-year-old woman, Cayce stated that her aura contained a warning regarding the possibility of an accident, causing him to recommend caution: "Before giving the Physical we would give a warning here as indicated in the aura of the body, [{*Ms.*} 1300]. Beware or be careful of an accident in something *moving*—as in elevator or cab." (1300-2)

Over the years Edgar Cayce provided many readings and suggestions for individuals to enhance their own intuition. While examining the ways in which psychic ability might manifest, the readings state that intuition can be heightened by subjugating material thoughts and influences to the soul self, such as through the use of prayer, meditation, the imagination, and personal reverie. In this type of state, which on one extreme might be similar to a literal trance and on the other extreme might simply involve an increase in the imaginative and intuitive forces, the mind could experience heightened psychic ability. This heightened intuition could be demonstrated, for example, in the ability of individuals to look into the past as well as to see the human aura. (507–1)

On frequent occasions Cayce suggested that each individual's aura has an affinity to specific colors—an affinity that causes the person to feel more comfortable or in sync with people, situations, and even the environment. Throughout the years he gave readings, one of the questions generally included with "color affinity" in mind was something along the lines of: "To what color do I best vibrate?" For example, when a thirty-six-year-old restaurant owner asked, "To what color or colors do I vibrate?" Cayce replied, "Blue. And when wearing blue you won't get mad! And make much of these in the underthings, too, close to the body." (594–1) In other words, the reading suggested that the color blue would provide her with a vibration (even when worn as underwear) that would help her in controlling her own temper. On another occasion a teenage girl who was both deaf and mute went to Cayce for physical assistance. In addition to recommending some more conventional health protocols, he encouraged the parents to let her work with stringed musical instruments so that she could "feel the vibration," as well as to keep two specific colors on her body and in her surroundings—deep violet and red. (4223–3) The colors were recommended because of the specific vibrations associated with each. Throughout the readings the vibration of red is often associated with energy and deep violet corresponds to higher states of consciousness, spiritual attunement, and healing.

Color and music were also recommended for a five-year-old boy to his parents who were looking for guidance on raising their child. During the course of their reading, Cayce outlined what kinds of music and colors the child would be drawn to and how the parents could use these in the boy's life as he grew older:

> One that, it will be found, music, musical tendencies, will be

> an influence in the entity's activities. The music will be *quieting, especially* that of stringed instruments—yet those of the horn, or pipe, or reed, will *later* be a more active influence in the entity's experience.
>
> *Colors* will also find an influence in the entity's activities, especially those of not too severe, but the violet, ultra-violet, shades of green, of mode [light/drab bluish-gray?], and pink; though the others may make for a rigor oft in the entity, the delicate shades—or those as may be termed the spiritual—will influence the entity. When illness or the like were to come about, soft music and the lighter shades or tones will quiet where medicine would fail. *773-1*

In addition to present-life information on colors and the aura, the Cayce material also examines both subjects in the context of reincarnation and past lives. For example, the readings state that previous experiences in the earth could be seen in " . . . *feelings* towards places, conditions, individuals . . . ," all containing an energy that was visible in the aura. (2067-1) Cayce also discussed how the influence of color and the desire to use color frequently resided in consciousness as a carryover from previous lifetimes.

As one case in point, a twenty-seven-year-old speaker and designer was told that during a previous lifetime in Egypt she had been in service to one of the temples. Her role there was to assist individuals in understanding their life's expression and purpose by working with colors and the aura. The reading encouraged her to read everything she could find on the subjects. It also advised her that the best information and knowledge she would have at her disposal would be obtained through working with auras and colors in her present experiences and practice, just as she had once done in the ancient past. In the language of the readings: "For there the entity gained the abilities to make for the harmonizing colors to those extents wherein each individual was and is as yet clothed with *its* individual color—as ye call aura." (1436-2)

She was encouraged to expand her work with color in lecturing on the subject, such as she might be able to accomplish on radio, as well as to become involved with the motion picture industry and the use of color in film. She was heartened with the statement that she could bring an understanding of the importance of color to others from both a metaphysical and a practical standpoint. When she asked specifically, "Am I fitted to do some special work in the new science of color?" the answer came:

> As we find and as has been indicated, that so far as the commercial field is concerned, associated with the new color for the cinema—these are the fields of activity in which the entity may make the application of the abilities for the means of the world.
>
> As for colors pertaining to life itself—as the self or the entity set in motion, *study* auras and aid *others* in knowing what they mean! There are those that interpret same in the form of spiritism. There are those that interpret same in the form of vibration. They are *all* of these and more, as the entity *knows* and may *experience!*
>
> Hence the studies that the entity may make will give, again, again, that leaven that leaveneth the whole, for the *use* of the masses in their *daily* experience! 1436-2

During a follow-up reading the woman mentioned that she had become interested in talking about the use of color to enhance beauty and charm and thought that might lead to working with both radio and the motion picture industry. Cayce reassured her that she was going in the right direction. When she asked what specific studies she should undertake regarding color, the reply indicated that studying color was ultimately the study of the self:

> *First* study *self!* in relationship to the Creative Forces, as has been the direction. Or the study of auras as related to the individual life, the individual expression in others. For this, as has been pointed out, was the greater portion of the physical activity in the material plane for giving out by the entity during the Egyptian period.
>
> Hence this as applied to material things, or as to commer-

> cial value within self, becomes the means, the manners, the way through which this may be given out the most. 1436-3

The reading went on to indicate that she needed to continue learning about the human aura, including comprehending how the daily activities of each individual affected the aura. Cayce suggested that realizing the connection among the body, an individual's activities, and the aura was central to truly understanding the subject: " . . . First learn the basic forces or basic principles of same as related to the bodily forces . . . learn the activity of the etheronic and the vibrations of the body, for these are they that produce color, that produce aura, that produce the activities seen *as* color." (1436-3) Once she truly understood auras at this level, she would be led to the next steps in fulfilling her own life's work.

Although it was never explored in greater detail and no one among Cayce's contemporaries asked for additional information on the subject, the readings also suggested that—in addition to the impact of colors upon individuals—each city actually possessed a unique vibration and hence a color with which it would be most in harmony. The concept occurred while Edgar Cayce was having a dream in which, while floating above the United States, he perceived himself peering down on various kinds of energies that seemed to be radiating from different areas of the country. He became aware of the fact that each of these energies was associated with different types of vibrations. In his dream, one area or city seemed to be radiating a vibration that was associated with health or healing, for example, while another seemed to be more closely aligned with commerce.[4] (294-131) Cayce briefly referred to the fact that each city possessed a corresponding color in a reading given to a twenty-nine-year-old woman. While tuning into the time and location of her birth (New York City), the reading stated simply: " . . . And each city has its own color!" (1456-1) He further broadened this concept in a different reading when he stated that even the planets have a corresponding color: " . . . For it is not strange that music, color, vibration

[4]For a discussion of Cayce and vibrations, see *Edgar Cayce on Vibrations* by Kevin J. Todeschi (Virginia Beach, VA: A.R.E. Press, 2007).

are all a part of the planets, just as the planets are a part—and a pattern—of the whole universe . . . " (5755-1)

This interconnectedness between color, music and vibration was mentioned again in a reading given to a twenty-three-year-old musician, who was told in part:

> As there is the music of the spheres, there is indeed the music of the growing things in nature. There is then the music of *nature* itself! There is the music of the growth of the rose, of *every* plant that bears color, of every one that opens its blossom for the edification, for the sanctification even of the environs thereabout! 949-12

A further exploration of music, vibration, sound, and color (and their healing properties) was discussed in the reading for a forty-one-year-old osteopath, who was apparently drawn to music:

> Yet music is a higher realm to the entity. And it may be found in the experience of the entity, as from those activities in the experience before this, that sounds, music and colors may have much to do with creating the proper vibrations about individuals that are mentally unbalanced, physically deficient or ill in body and mind; and may be used as helpful experiences . . . 1334-1

Perhaps one of the topics related to the human aura that is most unique to the Edgar Cayce information is his discussion of the "aurascope." Although it was mentioned in only four readings given to the same individual (440-3, 440-6, 440-7, and 440-12), the possibilities for this device are quite fascinating. Essentially, the readings described the aurascope as a hand-held machine, a little larger than binoculars, that would make it possible to see the aura around other people. The readings on the aurascope were given to a twenty-three-year-old student and electrical engineer interested in vibrations and energy fields. Since from Cayce's perspective, the aura is a vibrational energy field that emanates from all living things, the aurascope was basically a tool for measuring and seeing that energy.

According to the Cayce information, this machine would enable individuals with any degree of psychic ability to see another person's aura and diagnose that individual's physical, mental, and spiritual well-being. The following is how the readings discussed the theory behind the aurascope device and its ability to perceive vibrations and various colors (suggesting the health, well-being, state of mind, and more):

> As suggested, the theory of the mechanical device is to determine not only the aura of individuals but to use same in the diagnoses of disorders in various portions of the body.
>
> As is known, the body in action—or a live body—emanates from same the vibrations to which it as a body is vibrating, both physical and spiritual. Just as there is an aura when a string of a musical instrument is vibrated—the tone is produced by the vibration. In the body the tone is given off rather in the higher vibration, or the color. Hence this is a condition that exists with each physical body . . . 440-6

According to notations on file in the Cayce archives, over the years several individuals followed the instructions that were provided by the readings for creating an aurascope. Several prototypes have been created; however, no fully working model of this particular appliance has ever been produced.

Certainly Edgar Cayce himself was able to describe the aura while in his conscious state. In addition to his own experiences seeing the aura (see Appendix I—*Auras*), there are numerous examples of what he told individuals about their own auras. One of the best records of his conscious aura perception occurred during one of his Tuesday night Bible classes when he went around the room and described the auras that he saw for each of those present. His secretary, Gladys Davis, made note of all of his commentary. What follows is a selection of some of his descriptions:

To a thirty-six-year-old woman: "You have a great deal of violet, pink and white. The white means purity, always. Yours runs up and down, so you are rather temperamental. Everything to you must be very definite, must be very sure, with a basis that is sound."

To a twenty-eight-year-old man: "You have a great deal of blue, a great deal of gray—because you easily become discouraged at times. You go very much up and down; you will fly off the handle or fly on the handle just about as easy."

To a twenty-two-year-old woman: "You have a great deal of rose, and it becomes a very pretty aura. You judge most things by the material results that you get. I don't mean that you haven't any spirituality, but there is more of rose in your aura than the other colors. It changes, as rose would—or in coral—the changes sort of dash in and out. You smear it over, and then you streak it white and smear it over; then there's a streak of blue and you smear it over. That's the way you work."

And, to a thirty-six-year-old man: "You have more violet in your aura than anyone in the room. Violet always indicates the seeker, the searcher for something. You have more of [violet] than gray, blue, opal, white or pink. A great deal of pink or coral in an individual's aura indicates material-mindedness."

(See Appendix II: Examples of Edgar Cayce's Waking Aura Descriptions.)

Overall, the readings discussed color and auras as additional tools that could be used for better understanding the self. From Cayce's perspective, both provide a pictorial representation of an individual's energy, health, state of mind, thoughts, possibilities, and potentials. The aura contains information related to a person's talents, weaknesses, karmic lessons, and past lives. In a very real sense it is a barometer of the whole person—a gauge of one's physical, mental, emotional, and spiritual state of being. The Edgar Cayce readings declare that we are much more than a physical body and that we are connected to light, energy, color, and vibration. Perhaps the aura is an indicator of the nature of who we really are in ways that we have not yet dared to imagine.

2 The Vibration of Color

Science has demonstrated that color is basically our collective perception of the effects of wavelength and frequency. The Edgar Cayce material certainly agrees with this idea. The readings affirm that the various colors and tones we observe are associated with the way in which we perceive different rates of vibration. Going a step further, the Cayce material states that color is essentially the result of the manifested vibrations of spiritual energy. In fact, the readings detail the way in which personal spirituality impacts the aura, colors, and personal vibrations; and many readings explore the connection between spiritual growth, the evolution of personal vibration, and the specific colors associated with various levels of consciousness. From his own conscious state, Cayce described auras as follows:

> An aura is an effect, not a cause. Every atom, every molecule,

> every group of atoms and molecules—however simple or complex, however large or small—tells the story of itself, its pattern, its purpose, through the vibrations which emanate from it. Colors are the perceptions of these vibrations by the human eye. As the souls of individuals travel through the realms of being, they shift and change their patterns as they use or abuse the opportunities presented to them. Thus at any time, in any world, a soul will give off through vibrations the story of itself and the condition in which it now exists. If another consciousness can apprehend those vibrations, and understand them, it will know the state of its fellow being, the plight he is in, or the progress he has made. (See *Auras* booklet, Appendix I)

In addition to his conscious perceptions regarding the aura, many of Edgar Cayce's readings also describe this vibrational energy field in greater detail. There are also hundreds of readings that examine the connection between spiritual growth and consciousness development. When a group of Cayce's contemporaries asked for readings on the process of psychic development, the readings suggested instead that the real goal should become one of spiritual development which would, in turn, facilitate intuitive development as a natural by-product. Two collections of these readings explore this premise in greater detail—the Study Group readings (known as the "262 series") and the Prayer Group readings (known as the "281 series"). This material proposes that as individuals grow in consciousness, they raise their own personal vibration and are able to perceive higher states of intuitive or spiritual awareness. For example, when a forty-one-year-old member of the study group asked for a dream interpretation reading in which she saw the aura of herself and her sister, Cayce told her that the dream was "a glimpse of self-awakening." (262-8) Her work with spiritual growth was facilitating her intuitive talents. Similarly, when a twenty-eight-year-old member of the prayer group had begun to frequently see flashes and shapes in her line of sight, Cayce informed her that she was seeing the "higher vibrations" and "spiritual forces" of higher levels of consciousness. He also stated that her growth in spiritual development was prompting the phenomenon of "beginning to see auras." Connecting this to her own spiritual transformation, he added: " . . . As life, light, and love with understanding—is reflected in self, so may there be seen those of the *same* reflection from others." (281-4)

As discussed previously the readings for the prayer group also explored the colors associated with each of the seven major spiritual centers or chakras, which Cayce correlated with seven endocrine glands in the physical body. Each of the colors may correspond with both a positive and a negative level of consciousness.

Chakra/ Spiritual Center/Gland	Color	Positive Expression	Negative Expression
1. Gonads	Red	Energetic; productive; serves others; committed	Angry; self-indulgent; aggressive, prone to anxiety
2. Cells of Leydig	Orange	Balanced; creative; personally vital	Imbalanced; over- or undersexed; inflexible
3. Adrenals	Yellow	Intelligent; optimistic; thoughtful; forgiving; perceptive	Impractical; a dreamer; imbalance between heart and head
4. Thymus	Green	Loves others; innate healer; generous	Selfish; envious; jealous
5. Thyroid	Blue	Spiritual; willing to work with the Divine; cooperative	Indecisive or willful; idealistic versus realistic; judgmental; arrogant
6. Pineal	Indigo	Spiritually wise; intuitive; personal awareness of the Divine	Too self-sufficient
7. Pituitary	Violet	Spiritual; divine love; oneness	Self-righteous

Cayce reminded the prayer group: " . . . vibration is the essence or the basis of color . . . " (281-30) and stated that the color and energetic vibration associated with each of these levels of awareness would come to consciousness through practices such as meditation. Various approaches to personal relaxation can also help to elicit intuitive experiences. The rationale is that relaxation can enable the individual to set aside the personality self and draw instead upon attributes of the real soul self, which remains in tune with higher levels of consciousness.

Ironically, Cayce once told a thirty-four-year-old female artist who was extremely intuitive that one of her greatest challenges was her vibration. It was so high that she often had a hard time trying to understand and empathize with others. He suggested lowering her own vibration " . . . sufficient to comprehend the needs of many . . . " through the use of her artwork. His recommendation was to attune to others and to create drawings that would utilize color and harmony depicting their daily activities and concerns in a way that would provide inspiration. Cayce advised that she " . . . *become* the colors as well as the forms depicted." (2450-1) The premise in the readings is that an individual's consciousness grows and expands, which enables that person to see higher states of consciousness. That development of consciousness allows an individual to better assist people displaying diverse levels of personal development.

When a twenty-seven-year-old man asked for more information on what an aura was as well as what the specific colors signified, Cayce replied that the aura was essentially the vibratory "emanation" that surrounded an individual and changed continually, based upon the influences, activities, and ideas with which the individual was involved. The reading went on to describe the man's own aura and provided additional information for using both the intellectual mind and the intuitive mind working together as a means of developing his own psychic ability:

> For the self, as we find . . . *{the color is predominately} blue* . . . and is that of a *seeker;* indicating the geniality, pleasantness, the abilities to often pour oil upon troubled waters and quietness ensues with the advent of the body-

> consciousness into associations of most every nature or kind, and these—consequently—are well, and well to be cultivated.
>
> Aura changes, to be sure, to the *temperament*. Just as we may see, iron may be heated to hot; it also may be heated to white heat. The vibrations, see?
>
> (Q) Give detailed directions for developing the intuitive sense.
>
> (A) Trust more and more upon that which may be from within. Or, this is a very common—but a very definite—manner to develop:
>
> On any question that arises, ask the mental self—get the answer, yes or no. Rest on that. Do not act immediately (if you would develop the intuitive influences). Then, in meditation or prayer, when looking within self, ask—is this yes or no? The answer is intuitive development. On the same question, to be sure, see? 282-4

Understanding the connection between spiritual growth and intuitive development is important. When Carol Ann Liaros was directing the Project Blind Awareness program, she would have the program volunteers arrive a half hour early to form a circle and meditate on raising the vibrations within the room in which the program met. According to Carol Ann, "When the blind arrived, their energy fields would immediately be raised to a higher vibration. The results of our efforts were verified over and over again by the feelings of love that emanated from the participants."

As one means of testing the vibration of color Carol Ann Liaros and the volunteers of Project Blind Awareness devised a study working with local blind associations and Professor Douglas Dean, an electrochemist and parapsychologist at the New Jersey Institute of Technology. Twenty blind participants were recruited and put through one hundred color selection trials both before and after they had undergone twenty hours of Project Blind Awareness training. During these seasons, the blind participants were asked to run their hands over various colored sheets while the following questions were asked:

a) Did the colored sheets feel the same or different?
b) Could the blind individual differentiate between black and white?
c) Could the blind individual differentiate between red and blue?
d) Could the blind individual differentiate between a set of black and white sheets and a set of red and blue?

Because each individual participated in one hundred color selection trials, and because the laws of chance would entail a fifty-fifty "guess" on items a–c, and a 25 percent "guess" on item d, just by chance the following collective accuracy score would occur:

Anticipated participant scores based on the laws of chance:

	Same-Different Test	Black-White Test	Red-Blue Test	Black-White Red-Blue Test
TOTALS	1000	1000	1000	500

True enough, after the first one hundred color selection trials and prior to undertaking the intuitive training, the blind participants scored within the range of chance, as follows:

Participant scores prior to Project Blind Awareness training:

	Same-Different Test	Black-White Test	Red-Blue Test	Black-White Red-Blue Test
TOTALS	1028	1021	1028	523

Over the next seven weeks the participants were led through a series of exercises for both relaxation and intuitive development. At the end of the training a number of the participants reported being able to "see" in a way they could not quite verbalize or even totally understand. Some reported the ability to distinguish colors from across the room. Others said that they could perceive the outline of objects in a room. When asked to point to where they were perceiving color—as it could not have been visually—they usually pointed to their foreheads. Many of the subjects reported an increase in mobility because they began to "just know" where objects were in a room.

One man reported that he could walk down the street without a cane because he could "see" the plate glass windows, lamp posts, and more. Another woman stated that she was able to pick out her clothes from her closet because she could "tell the difference" in colors by running her hands over the clothing at a distance of several inches. Another woman described her new abilities, as follows: "An awareness of my own energy field is developing and I feel as though I really see myself: I see my hands working, I see my body, I see images and shadows, and seem to be able to almost see what is in a room. It seems that I really see it, although I can't, as I am totally blind. Last Sunday I saw my first aura. A friend was talking with me when suddenly I saw her aura and was so surprised that I did not hear what she was saying. She noticed that I was not listening and said that my eyes got larger and larger until she knew that something was going on. I interrupted her and said, 'I can see your aura.' It was a white light, hazy and flickering, which encircled her head."

In an interesting incident, one of the blind participants was scanning the aura of her volunteer and was commenting about heat, coolness, and other descriptions as she scanned. When she progressed to the feet and passed her hand over one part of the left foot, she reported, "Oh, it feels very cool here." Much to the blind woman's shock, her volunteer replied, "Yes! That's right. I had a toe removed several years ago!" A similar experience was noted in a sixty-two-year-old blind student who became astonished when she scanned the aura of her volunteer and noticed how cold it felt in the torso area. The volunteer told her that she had undergone a hysterectomy!

Carol Ann Liaros had her own experience with the blind participants that she describes, as follows:

> All of the lights were off in the room where the group met. I was standing up against a white wall for an exercise in which I was encouraging the blind participants to practice "seeing" my aura. (Many were having experiences of seeing through their foreheads.) Several comments were made by participants about the colors when suddenly many in the group declared

that they saw red in my aura way up high to my left. I couldn't understand why so many of them were seeing red. I certainly wasn't feeling angry or mad, and red is often the color of anger in the aura.

Later, the lights were turned on and we were on our break. I happened to look up at the wall where so many of them had indicated that they could see red in my aura, and I laughed. There was an EXIT sign there. It was not an illuminated sign, but painted red on the wall, and I had not seen it when the lights were out!

From a research point of view, perhaps the next results were the most amazing. After the seven-week period of training, participants again took the one hundred color selection trials; and this time their scores measured far beyond the laws of chance:

Participant scores after 20 hours of Project Blind Awareness training[5]:

	Same-Different Test	Black-White Test	Red-Blue Test	Black-White Red-Blue Test
TOTALS	1649	1316	1348	835

In the period of more than forty years that Carol Ann Liaros has been leading intuition training exercises, many very interesting experiences have occurred with participants (both sighted and blind). Stories like these suggest that color and vibration are somehow quantifiable for those who have firsthand experience and knowledge with intuitive perception:

- Bobby was a nine-year-old blind child with no light perception. His lack of sight had been discovered a couple of months after his birth. A participant in the Junior Project Blind Awareness program, one of the exercises geared for children was to have them lie on large colored sheets (squares, approximately three feet long

[5]Agatha P. Tutko, "Teaching the Blind to See," *Fate* Magazine (May 1975).

on each side) and "feel" the vibration of the color. The sheets contained colors from the following colors: red, yellow, green, blue, white, and black.

- Each child was encouraged to lie down on a colored sheet and to stretch out his or her entire body, enabling the body to feel the color's vibration. They were encouraged to feel the color with their hands, elbows, nose, bottom of feet, and so forth, and then describe the color to their volunteer. (All of the volunteers in the youth program were school teachers.) The children were told that with practice they should be able to recognize the various colors by the physical sensation they were experiencing. Bobby was doing fine with the colors until he lay down on the color black. As soon as he was on the ground, he immediately jumped to his feet and said, "I don't like that color! It reminds me of my father's funeral."
- Sam was a blind adult whose eyes had been removed because of cancer. After taking some ESP classes and working with his intuition, he described the ability to see auras through the middle of his forehead. One of the talents he demonstrated was identifying dark spots in different people's auras that accurately corresponded to areas of physical problems. During one of the classes, a young, sighted woman asked Sam to look at her aura and describe what he saw. He briefly described her aura and then hesitated, as though he was uncomfortable and ill-at-ease. When he was pressed to share what he was seeing, Sam replied, "I see two auras! Is she pregnant?" Interestingly enough, the young woman had just found out that she was about four weeks pregnant. When he was asked to specify whether the child was a boy or a girl, Sam leaned forward as if he was trying to see better and stated assuredly, "It's a boy." Several months later the woman delivered a beautiful baby boy.
- During one of the basic ESP classes that included experiencing the human aura, participants had taken turns having their auras described by the rest of the class. After the class had looked at the auras of four or five individuals, one of the students who was in his mid-twenties walked forward and stood up against the white

wall. No one was able to see the man's aura. Even Carol Ann was unable to see his aura. Carol Ann passed it off as: "everyone's eyes are tired." She was baffled as it was an experience she had not previously encountered. The reason for the group's experience became clear when class started the following week. One of the students brought in a newspaper article about a young mailman that had been killed while delivering mail in the rural countryside in his small mail truck. The truck had somehow hit a cow, rolled over, and the mailman had died in the accident. The mailman had been the student in the class whose aura could not be seen! This experience is certainly reminiscent of something Edgar Cayce had to say about the human aura:

> Where do the colors come from, and what makes them shift and change? Well, color seems to be a characteristic of the vibration of matter, and our souls seem to reflect it in this three-dimensional world through atomic patterns. We are patterns, and we project colors, which are there to those who can see them. Apparently the aura reflects the vibrations of the soul. *When a person is marked for death the soul begins to withdraw and the aura naturally fades.* (Authors' emphasis; See *Auras booklet*, Appendix I)

On one occasion a twenty-nine-year-old businessman asked Edgar Cayce to describe the vibrations that emanated from the human aura. Cayce's answer once again connected the aura with the effect of the vibration of an individual's spiritual attunement and life experience. When the man asked specifically whether the vibrations of an aura were measurable in terms of frequency and wavelength (such as a light wave), Cayce responded: "May be compared to same, but of the spiritual radiation {*emanation*}, and not material radiation {*emanation*}; that is, those radiations {*emanations*} as come from spirit form may take form in vibratory radiation {*emanation*} of color, or light, through the individual's attunement." (900–22) {*Authors' note: Cayce is describing "emanation" not radiation as it is generally used in modern-day terminology.*} Eight years later Cayce told the same individual that " . . . All vibration, see, produces color . . . "

(900–149) At the time, the businessman had sought a series of dream interpretation readings and noted how he was seeing various shades of color in his dreams. Cayce confirmed that these colors were associated with different levels of vibration and consciousness and that, in general, denser colors would correspond to things that were more physical whereas the lighter colors would be related to the higher realms of consciousness and spirituality.

On another occasion Cayce told a twenty-year-old woman interested in art, symbolism, and color that colors within an aura emanate as vibrations from an individual based on that individual's activities, thoughts, and personality. Cayce added that each of these colors " . . . indicates the step of {*an individual's*} development . . . ," (275–30) making it possible to see every influence that was a part of the individual's being, ranging from the purely carnal to the higher spiritual developments. Later, Cayce described the woman's aura as being "blue to purple." When she asked for follow-up information on the color of her aura, it included the following:

> (Q) What is the meaning of my aura, blue to purple?
> (A) As the color or tone indicates, the blue in purity and the purple towards spirituality.
> (Q) What are the best colors for me to wear?
> (A) Blue, and those tones or shades that go toward the deep or royal purple, and the modes that are in between. Not decided figures or stripes are well for body.
> (Q) What colors should surround me?
> (A) Those of gold and blue are healing colors, as is purple, for the body.
> (Q) What precious stone sends out the most healing vibrations for my body?
> (A) Those of the pearl and of the bloodstone. 275-31

In other places in the readings, Cayce described personal spirituality as being best attained through three ongoing practices—working with spiritual ideals, working with personal application, and working with personal attunement. In a variety of readings given to individuals over a period of many decades, these same tools were described as being instrumental in enhancing personal intuition and improving one's ability to perceive various levels of consciousness.

There is a complex interaction between consciousness, vibration, and color. In terms of consciousness, an individual is able to perceive various levels of awareness based upon his or her own level of spiritual development and personal vibration. In terms of vibration, both consciousness and color have a corresponding vibration—the higher an individual's vibration, the higher the corresponding level of consciousness. In addition, the higher an individual's vibration, the more frequently he or she can attune to the needs and consciousness of others. In terms of color, each color has a corresponding vibration based upon its wavelength and frequency.

From the standpoint of the Edgar Cayce information, each individual's being is a complex combination of all personal activity, thought, belief, bias, and desire. In the language of the readings, " . . . each soul-entity is a combination of all this it has been . . . " (294-204) These urges and inclinations constitute both consciousness and vibration, and their effects can literally be perceived as color in the human aura. In simplest terms, thoughts and activities somehow have a physical manifestation. From this perspective the aura is essentially a vibration of the whole self—a vibration that manifests in various colors. Each of these colors has a corresponding meaning for all those who have the ability to see.

3 The Meaning of Colors (Red, Orange, and Yellow)

Red

One of the ways that individuals can begin to decipher the possible meanings of colors in the human aura is to look for clues in everyday language. Statements such as "I was so mad I saw red," "He was green with envy," "She has a green thumb," "She is worth her weight in gold," "He has a heart of gold," "They are both stick-in-the-muds (brown)," "He always has a black mood," "Pale as death," "She is as bright as the sun (yellow)," "He is certainly grounded (brown)," "She has a mercurial personality (silver is erratic and unpredictable)," and so forth, have important meaning. These language clues can be extremely helpful, especially for those who are beginning to compile their own comprehension of the possible meaning of colors.

Another approach that may be used to explore color is to look up the definitions in an unabridged dictionary, which often lists metaphorical expressions used in contemporary language. For example, "white as snow" may be associated with purity; and "she lives in an ivory tower" may suggest one who is aloof and detached. A third approach is personal experience—beginning to see your own colors. Through your experiences, begin to decipher and understand what those colors may mean to you. A fourth approach is to look into the possible meanings of colors cited by others who can see the human aura. For example, Carol Ann Liaros recalls the following in terms of her own experiences in seeing the color red:

> When my son was involved in sports when he was younger, I noticed that the children had different amounts of red (clear, vibrant red) in their auras. The most active, energetic ones were usually the most successful in that particular sport. However, seeing my daughter's aura when she was mad at me for grounding her was different. The aura of red daggers coming from her neck had a slight scarlet edge or cast to it. While there was lots of energy, there was also anger mixed with it.

In terms of Edgar Cayce's personal experiences, Cayce noted the following regarding red:

> Red is the first of the primary colors and in ancient symbolism it represented the body, the earth, and hell, all three of which meant the same thing in the old mystery religions. The earth was the irrational world into which the soul descended from heaven . . .
>
> As to the meaning of red, it indicates force, vigor and energy. Its interpretation depends upon the shade, and as with all colors, upon the relationship of other colors. Dark red indicates high temper, and it is a symbol of nervous turmoil. A person with dark red in his aura may not be weak outwardly, but he is suffering in some way, and it is reflected

> in his nervous system. Such a person is apt to be domineering and quick to act. If the shade of red is light it indicates a nervous, impulsive, very active person, one who is probably self-centered. Scarlet indicates an overdose of ego. Pink or coral, is the color of immaturity. It is seen usually in young people, and if it shows up in the aura of one who is grown, it indicates delayed adolescence, a childish concern with self. In all cases of red, there is a tendency to nervous troubles, and such people ought to take time to be quiet and to get outside themselves.
>
> Red is the color of the planet Mars, and corresponds *{vibrationally}* to Do, the first note in the musical scale. In early Christianity it signified the suffering and death of Christ, and was the color of war, strife, and sacrifice. (See *Auras* booklet, Appendix I)

The Cayce archives also contain the following "waking" aura descriptions that Edgar Cayce cited regarding red: "There's been a great deal of red about you lately, which means that you've been rather defiant . . . " (288-31, Report #18) Other conscious notations in the files are as follows:

> [1467]: Your aura is very, very definite; it has changed since I've known you, as much as anyone I've ever seen. Your aura is a sort of crown, but in the form of long spikes that go up—and that are of varied colors. Sometimes the colors run from one shade to another; they might become very red and then very pink all along. Because you go up to the heights and then down to the depths. But you have a very good aura."
>
> [2175]: Yours changes almost according to your moods. So you know about how many colors it would take. It effervesces; then you almost rub it out at times, in streaks; indicating those ideals that are your determining factors from sober thinking, and never snap judgments. When you really act on a thing you give sober judgment and thought to it. You make decisions by second thought. You flare into a thing and

> then you think it over. It's a mighty good thing to do, especially since there is not so much red in your aura. You don't act on things when you are mad, which is about as nice a thing as can be said about anybody. You may do something when you are mad, but you don't really mean it.
>
> 5746-1, Report #2

Red was also a topic of discussion in the Cayce readings. For example, when a forty-five-year-old stenographer obtained additional information about her life's purpose and her soul's strengths and weaknesses, Cayce recommended that she begin using "very red stones," such as that made of coral, which she could use as a belt, necklace, or bracelet. Apparently the individual had quite a number of challenges and "tumultuous conditions" in her life. Cayce advised that the vibrations from these red stones would help bring "more of harmony into the experience of the entity in the present activity." She was also encouraged to wear clothing that contained the color blue, especially when she slept, as the vibration of the color would help to quiet her mind. In terms of general guidance and advice, her reading offered the following:

> . . . And if a body-mind, a body-physical, a soul-body would have understanding, then *give*—that it may have. For they that would have life, love, hope, faith, brotherly love, kindness, gentleness, mercy, must *show* these things in their relationships to those they meet in every walk of life. Dare to speak gently, when even thine self is troubled. Dare to speak gently when thou art even berated by those from whom, in the *material* sense, ye have every right to expect or to even demand honor, and hope, and faith. Though they act in the opposite, with these environs about self as intimated the entity will be able to meet such; not as omens, not as good luck, but as facts for thine *own* development. For thy soul has been tried as by fire through many of thine experiences in the earth . . . Hence the red, the deep red coral, upon thine flesh, will bring quietness in those turmoils that have arisen within

> the inner self; as also will the pigments of blue to the body bring the air, the fragrance of love, mercy, truth and justice that is within self. 694-2

During a reading given for a woman suffering from anemia and chronic fatigue, Cayce recommended the color "red and the shades of same" as those colors most in alignment with her personal vibration. (574-1) Because red can be associated with energy and vitality, the vibration of the color would obviously help the woman overcome her exhaustion and lack of vigor.

On another occasion, a forty-four-year-old woman who was extremely sensitive and possessed a great deal of intuition was told that many of her challenges were due to the fact that she frequently went against her own intuition, creating a great deal of personal turmoil in the process. She was encouraged to have upon her person stones that were red (such as a ruby or bloodstone), as they would help her to follow her own guidance. Rather than seeing the stones as some kind of charm or magic, the reading counseled:

> These as we find are as influences; not that these *bring* conditions to pass, but they are channels, vibrations that are created about the entity that may have their impression upon the imaginative forces and influence them within the entity for greater or better activity. 1616-1

Elsewhere in the readings, the energetic vibrations of bloodstone and ruby were explained to a forty-nine-year-old retired concert singer as tools for helping individuals apply constructive thought in creative endeavors. (1770-2) This woman was also encouraged to keep such stones on or about her body at all times for their helpful influence.

Parents of a fifteen-year-old-boy were advised to give their son things that were "coral red." The color was recommended as a means of helping to balance the young man's "emotional urges," as well as his overly-sensitive temperament. The youth was supersensitive to things of a psychic nature, and Cayce stated that the boy would respond to red as it would also provide a balance to his conflicting emotions. (963-1)

Red was a prominent color recommended in the reading given for a nineteen-year-old student interested in the arts. In addition to recommending clothing that contained "a great deal of color," Cayce suggested that the young woman obtain and wear a ruby, presumably for its color and vibration. A closer look at the individual's life reading suggests that the energy of red may have been recommended for emotional stability and grounding, as the young woman was warned against being in any situation that caused "contention." In previous incarnations she had also had challenges with personal fears, a lack of determination, and an inability to deal with practical financial concerns in the material world. In terms of her innate strengths, the reading provided the following: "In the field of activity as a critic of books, of plays, of manuscripts, of tenets, of teachings, may be a channel through which the entity may given expression—as well as in the home." (1891-1) Years later after Edgar Cayce's death, the woman's mother wrote a follow-up report to Cayce's organization (the A.R.E.) in which she stated, " . . . My daughter [1891] was told to wear a ruby stone which she has done ever since . . . "

In the case of a twenty-three-year-old man suffering from severe eye problems and lesions, Cayce advised him to wear shaded lenses the color of rose or amber-rose and to see a specialist. The reading stated that consistently wearing the colored lenses would help to break up the lesions. (1132-1)

In March 1929, more than six months before the great Stock Market Crash, a thirty-year-old stock broker had a dream in which he "got the impression regarding the market that we ought to sell everything." In the dream he saw a bull following a family member wearing a red dress. He tried to catch the bull but could not. Cayce stated that the dream was symbolic of the danger in the bull market and was also an indication that there would be a "considerable break" in the market unless stable banking conditions intervened in order to provide relief. Cayce told the individual that the dream was, in fact, a warning. In this case the red dress was symbolic of both warning and danger. (137-115 and 900-425)

Examples from Project Blind Awareness in regard to red include one participant named Bill who was attending a Knights of Columbus meeting with some friends. As Bill was seated and waiting with his friends a gentleman came up from behind and greeted them. When Bill turned to the person he asked, "Have you had a fight with your wife? Your aura is all red!" The individual was extremely surprised since he had indeed had a fight with his wife prior to the meeting. What was perhaps more surprising to the individual was the fact that Bill was completely blind with no light perception!

Another woman named Lola who had been blind for nearly thirty years due to Retinitis pigmentosa shocked her daughter on one occasion by saying, "What a beautiful red dress you're wearing!" Lola had somehow "felt" the vibration of the color even without seeing it—a frequent occurrence in the lives of many other blind participants in the Project Blind Awareness program.

Orange

In his *Auras* booklet, this is what Edgar Cayce had to say concerning the color orange:

> Orange is the color of the sun. It is vital, and a good color generally, indicating thoughtfulness and consideration of others. Again, however, it is a matter of shade. Golden orange is vital and indicates self-control, whereas brownish orange shows a lack of ambition and a don't care attitude. Such people may be repressed, but usually they are just lazy. People with orange in their auras are subject to kidney trouble.
>
> In the early church, orange signified glory, virtue, and the fruits of the earth, all of these being connected naturally with the sun. In the musical scales, the note Re corresponds to *{the vibration of}* orange. (See *Auras* booklet, Appendix I)

A waking description noted in the Cayce archives in regard to orange is the following: "[1222]: 'Your aura has changed a great deal in the last year or so. You have a great deal more of those colors that indicate sureness in self; orange with gold . . .'" (5746-1, Report #2)

The color orange was cited on one occasion when a family friend obtained a reading for a fourteen-year-old girl. The child was told that "conflicting conditions" in her life needed to be addressed for her own well-being and development. In part the young woman was hypersensitive and extremely intuitive, especially when it came to picking up on others psychically—their thoughts, their personal vibrations, even the vibrations of the colors they were wearing! Cayce told her, " . . . For the entity is not only able and capable to receive the vibrations of individuals about the entity as to their colors but as to their vibrations. And these then make for a sensitiveness that is often disturbing to the entity." (1406-1) Cayce acknowledged that this hypersensitivity had—up to this point—been a burden to the young woman; however, he said that she could either overcome this sensitivity or channel it in helpful directions for herself and others.

In terms of how it could be helpful, the reading advised her that whenever she saw "low" or "dark" red around people, she should consider it a danger sign or a warning about being involved with these individuals. She was also told that whenever she felt the vibration of orange, especially when it was orange mixed with violet hues, she was becoming somewhat melancholy, sentimental, and depressed. At that point she needed to focus her mind in other directions—directions that "make for a joy and an understanding." Cayce promised her that should she continue to work with her color and vibration sensitivity, in time she would come to know personally what specific vibrations and colors mean; and she would also know which individuals she could trust. He added that she would be especially connected to individuals whose predominant colors in the aura were "lighter red," "shades of green," and shades of green with "shadings into white."

In order to help ground her and improve her sensitivity she was encouraged to wear opals or moonstones "as a locket about the neck." She was also told that if she wore a pearl or opal ring it would enable her to experience the colors and vibrations of others with greater clarity. Ultimately Cayce suggested that her sensitivity and intuition could bring "into the experience of others a helpful, hopeful influence."

When the girl's parents asked about the direction of their child's life's work, the advice came that it would be in any field associated with intuition, teaching, or nursing. When the question was asked on behalf of the girl, "What particular psychic faculties should I attempt to develop . . . ?" The reply was, "As has been indicated, vibrations and color." (1406–1)

Rather than believing that the aura is constantly stable, case #452 from the Cayce files presents just one example of how the aura of each individual is in a constant state of change dependent upon the activities with which that person is involved. In November 1932 a twenty-eight-year-old protestant minister obtained a reading for his own personal and spiritual enlightenment and occupational direction. His ultimate goal was to find a position in which he could help supervise other ministers and missionaries. During the course of that reading he inquired as to what was the dominant color in his aura, and Cayce's response was, "Blue to violet." (452–6) Blue to violet is primarily associated with spiritual truths, things of a spiritual nature, and spiritual attainment.

One year later the minister obtained another reading, asking a series of additional questions about his life's purpose. Cayce confirmed his purpose was ultimately directed toward assisting ministers and missionaries to become of greater service to God and humankind. Since his last reading the individual had also begun to seriously consider the possibility of converting to Catholicism. He had met a young Catholic woman with whom he was interested in the possibility of marriage, and he was looking earnestly for more lucrative employment (most likely as a means of supporting a wife). When he asked about his aura's dominant color on this occasion Cayce replied that it was "high orange," indicating his recent focus as an intellectual "seeker." Cayce went on to say that if the young minister continued on his current path of focusing on the qualities of sincerity and consistency, the dominant color would transition to blues and greens. As noted blue is associated with spirituality, and green is often appropriate for those involved in any kind of healing or ministry work. (452–7)

Yellow

Yellow is described as follows in the Cayce booklet *Auras*::

> *{In ancient symbolism}* The mind was associated with yellow. It is interesting that in some systems of metaphysics blue is considered to be the true color of the sun; that is, if we could be outside earth we would see the sun as a blue light—soft, powerful and spiritual. The yellow color is supposed to result from the collision of the sun's rays with the atmosphere of earth. Since the greatest spiritual weapon of man is his intellect, it is natural that mind be associated with the sun's color in this world . . .
>
> Yellow is the second primary color. When it is golden yellow, it indicates health and well-being. Such people take good care of themselves, don't worry, and learn easily; good mentality is natural in them. They are happy, friendly, and helpful. If the yellow is ruddy, they are timid. If they are redheads, they are apt to have an inferiority complex. They are thus apt often to be indecisive and weak in will, inclined to let others lead them.
>
> In the musical scale the note Mi corresponds to *{the vibration of}* yellow, and Mercury is the planet of this color. (See *Auras* booklet, Appendix I)

The color yellow also figures prominently in the story of Father Schommer, an extremely intelligent Jesuit priest who possessed a high IQ, a photographic memory, and enough talent with the violin to play with the Buffalo Philharmonic Orchestra. Tragically Father Schommer was "blinded" twice. A disease blinded one eye, and the other eye was blinded during a round of golf when a stray golf ball hit him directly in the sighted eye. He joined Project Blind Awareness and became an enthusiastic participant.

One evening when the group was doing color scanning, one of the sighted volunteers noticed something unusual about Father Schommer's accuracy with the color scan exercise. The laminated color sheet was put on the table in front of Father Schommer. With his hand a few inches above the table the priest would scan a colored sheet and then verbalize his answer. The volunteer couldn't help but notice Father Schommer's own aura during the exercise: "It would bulge on one side of his head—a bright yellow—then he would speak." As the volunteer watched she noticed that whenever the aura bulged a bright yellow on the right side of the priest's head, his verbalized response about the color was correct. However, whenever the aura bulged on the left side of his head, the answer was incorrect. The volunteer determined that whenever Father Schommer "felt" the correct answer, the right side became dominant. When it was simply a guess the left side became dominant.

Long ago Carol Ann Liaros noted the predominance of yellow auras in some of her workshops:

> Many years ago while presenting a workshop, I noticed the auras above the attendees' heads were yellow and melded together to form somewhat of a group aura. Those who were "getting it" had auras that grew larger and were shinier than the others. When people had difficulty understanding or in some way did not "get it," their aura lost its shininess and began to get smaller—almost as if they were embarrassed and shrinking down in their seats even though they had not physically moved! When I noticed something like this had happened I gave the directions in a different manner or I tried to use other words to get across what I had been describing. By using different words I finally connected with those individuals, and they understood what I was explaining. As a result their auras became the same size and brightness as the rest of the group.
>
> Having learned this idea when I have taught groups of teachers who want to enhance their psychic abilities as a way of helping their students, I have suggested looking at the auras of their class and watching this phenomena. It can be tremendously helpful because there are students who are too shy or too embarrassed to admit that they don't understand.

It is just one more practical application of our psychic skills.

While giving a reading to a forty-three-year-old probation officer, Edgar Cayce stated that one of the colors his aura would respond to was yellow. Some of the qualities associated with yellow are the intellect, concentration, and the education of others. Interestingly enough, the man was told that in one of his most recent past lives he had been both a teacher and overseer to students of the settlers in his community. In addition to possessing an interest in the mental education of young people he also possessed from his own soul's past an innate love of history and literature—all associated with yellow in his aura. (478-1)

On another occasion, a Dr. [2120] asked Edgar Cayce why she had such a strong connection to colors. The response was that a strong affinity to color was often traceable to past lives when those colors were used for a particular purpose. Cayce told the woman who was an educator in the present that she had been a temple instructor in ancient Egypt, responsible for the education of women. During that period she had used colors as a means of signifying activities in the temple. She was especially fond of colors associated with opal and topaz (e.g.: yellow, orange, blue, red, etc.) and often made scarabs (miniature beetles) that individuals could hold and carry on their person.

In another instance from the Cayce files when a woman wrote to request a reading for her fourteen-year-old daughter, the woman complained about her daughter's disposition and stated, "My daughter, [3806], has given me considerable anxiety." Apparently the girl was extremely independent and defiant, causing one of the mother's questions to be why the girl was not more obedient with her mother and teachers. Part of Cayce's counsel was for the mother not to break the girl's will but instead to find ways to channel in more positive directions her determination to have her own way. The reading went on to suggest that sometimes the girl was correct in her determination, and part of the girl's independent nature could be traced to a life that she had lived among the Mormon pioneers who journeyed to Salt Lake City, Utah during the nineteenth century.

Cayce advised the girl's mother to buy her daughter an amethyst pendant necklace as it would help to normalize her temperament. Twice during the course of the reading he also suggested that the child wear yellow and blue colors, " . . . as {*the*} vibrations will make for the better environment for the body." (3806-1) Certainly yellow may be associated with the intellect and concentration, but the vibration may also help to dispel fear and worry in others (perhaps the mother?). In terms of blue, in addition to its connection to spirituality and wisdom, it also has an affinity to individuals with strong, self-reliant, and confident personalities.

4 The Meaning of Colors (Green, Blue, Indigo, and Violet)

Green

We often associate green with the expression "having a green thumb," spring and summer, growth, and even that which is healthy and alive. With these ideas in mind it should come as no surprise that green is often regarded as the color of health and vitality. According to Carol Ann Liaros it is often the color that corresponds with the healing professions: "The first time I saw a healer work on a subject, I noticed a beautiful green color all around the hands of the healer. After that, whenever I saw green around a client's hands, I would ask if the individual was in the healing professions in some way. The answer was always, 'yes!'" People practicing in the field of healing and health care—nurses, doctors, psychologists, spiritual healers, massage therapists, and so forth—tend to have some aspect of clear, beautiful green in their aura.

Edgar Cayce also saw the appearance of green as being related to healing. In his *Auras* booklet, he comments, as follows:

> Pure emerald green, particularly if it has a dash of blue, is the color of healing. It is helpful, strong, friendly. It is the color of doctors and nurses, who invariably have a lot of it in their auras. However, it is seldom a dominating color, usually being overshadowed by one of its neighbors. As it tends toward blue, it is more helpful and trustworthy. As it tends toward yellow, it is weakened. A lemony green, with a lot of yellow, is deceitful. As a rule the deep, healing green is seen in small amounts, but it is good to have a little of it in your aura.
>
> Saturn is the *{vibrational}* planet of this color, and Fa is its musical note. In the early church, it symbolized youthfulness and the fertility of nature, taking this quite naturally from the sight of the fields in spring. (See *Auras* booklet, Appendix I)

On one occasion Edgar Cayce informed a forty-seven-year-old woman that she had innate talents as a healer and could effectively help to heal individuals through prayer and the laying on of hands—a method in which a healer works with attunement and then directs healing energy through his or her hands. The readings suggested that this talent had been developed in ancient Persia, where she had once lived as a desert healer. With this in mind Cayce suggested that she would be drawn to blue-green " . . . as a color, as a vibration . . . ," (1469-1) and that these colors would also assist her in raising her personal vibration. He went on to state that she would know she was in attunement and ready to do her healing work when she saw a blue-green light. After the reading, the woman told Cayce's family and his secretary that she had definitely had experiences working with healing in the present—especially healing members of her own family—and that she always saw the blue-green light before she began.

A twenty-three-year-old male office clerk was encouraged to pursue the field of healing. Cayce stated, " . . . For even the aura of the entity is green, indicating those abilities towards healing. They run in streaks or lines not altogether parallel, but the abilities of the entity are indicated to meet same." (3545-1) It was a talent that he had apparently acquired during an incarnation in the Holy Land during the same time that the Apostle Paul was beginning his ministry. The reading encouraged him to pursue the work of healing again. Later when the individual asked about where he should work, the response came: "As just indicated, in the healing arts, especially in hydrotherapy and electrotherapy and massage."

In terms of the healing vibration of color, the Edgar Cayce information repeatedly recommended using an ultraviolet handheld light held against a green glass that was placed approximately fourteen inches from an area of the body in need of healing. Seen as a form of electrotherapy and healing vibration, the Cayce readings usually prescribed its use in conjunction with other treatments such as osteopathic adjustments or massage. For example, the ultraviolet light was recommended in the case of a fifty-seven-year-old woman who had a variety of circulation problems. When she complained about muscle stiffness, Cayce recommended massage followed by the use of the ultraviolet light:

> . . . While the body is resting after the massage, which it should do from twenty to thirty minutes at least, give the body the Ultra-Violet Light—with the Green Light projected between the Ultra-Violet and the body; for the healing effect that such, which in color and in radiation of the light, has upon the body-forces. 1567-4

The same treatment was recommended in the case of an eighteen-month-old toddler who had been diagnosed with an inoperable, malignant tumor. Cayce's rationale to the parents was as follows:

> . . . in most instances where there is needed a change in vibration, the projection of a green light is preferable—because green is the healing vibration. Here, in the character or nature of disturbance where there is the formation of that which is any malignant nature, the green light will be more

> effective than even that of a more penetrating nature, or even the x-ray—that destroys tissue . . . do not administer here other than the Ultra-Violet—the Mercury Light, with the green glass projected between the body and the Light. Have the Light at least thirty-seven to thirty-eight inches from the body, and the green glass about fourteen inches from the body. Use for only a minute and a half, about twice each week.
>
> 3370-1

Elsewhere Cayce recommended that a green lapis lazuli stone could be encased in glass and worn upon the body for general health. He went on to state that the vibration from this type of jewelry would even become a "healing influence to others" whenever they came near. (3416-1) Another reading also suggested that treatment facilities specializing in the health care field should always be painted in a range "between green and blue." (165-17)

Rather than being associated with healing, a fifty-year-old female legal assistant was told that for her, green was synonymous with jealousy. Although not completely explained, her reading did counsel that because something traumatic had happened to her in the long-ago past apparently on the date of June 15, at a very deep level one of her greatest ongoing fears was the "fear of what may come to pass," especially on that day. Cayce suggested that the fear was a memory residue from a past-life experience and was somehow specifically connected to an individual whose initials the woman gave in the present as "E.D.I." From the reading it appears as though this same individual had in the long-ago past been connected to her and then unexpectedly left her for another, causing the jealousy and fear that remained as memory within her being. When the woman asked about the possibility of getting in touch with Mr. "E.D.I." again, Cayce warned: "No! Best to let him alone. For these are {*the*} sources of fear . . . " (5030-1)

Blue

Edgar Cayce associated blue with elements regarded as possessing a spiritual nature:

> Blue has always been the color of the spirit, the symbol of contemplation, prayer, and heaven. The sky is blue because gas molecules in the air cause light rays from the sun to be scattered. This is the scientific explanation but, as I have mentioned before, blue is said to be the true color of the sun, and it is also the color of the planet Jupiter, which is the ruler of great thoughts and high-mindedness.
>
> Almost any kind of blue is good, but the deeper shades are the best. Pale blue indicates little depth, but a struggle toward maturity. The person may not be talented, but he tries. He will have many heartaches and many headaches, but he will keep going in the right direction. The middle blue, or aqua, belongs to a person who will work harder and get more done than the fellow with light blue, though there may be little difference between them in talent. Those with the deep blue have found their work and are immersed in it. They are apt to be moody and are almost always unusual persons, but they have a mission and they steadfastly go about fulfilling it. They are spiritual-minded for the most part, and their life is usually dedicated to an unselfish cause, such as science, art, or social service. I have seen many Sisters of Mercy with this dark blue, and many writers and singers also.
>
> The musical note of blue is Sol, and in the early church the color was assigned to the highest attainments of the soul. (See *Auras* booklet, Appendix I)

The importance of the color blue was cited in a dream interpretation reading given by Edgar Cayce to a twenty-one-year-old woman who was worried about her sick, hospitalized mother. Her mother had been hospitalized due to complications after an operation that the readings claimed had been unnecessary. The elder woman was apparently allergic to anesthesia in addition to having severe pressure in her head and ongoing complications with blood clots and popping blood vessels. Understandably the elder woman's daughter was extremely worried about her mother. In a dream the younger woman was wearing a blue and white dress and was kneeling before the doctor, as though praying or begging for help. The doctor patted her on the head as if to reassure her. A reading was given on the dream in which Cayce stated that the younger woman had done all she could possibly due to assist her mother. She was praying in the dream just as she had prayed for her mother in real life. The doctor represented the Great Physician (e.g., the Christ or God); and her blue and white dress was symbolic—according to Cayce—of her pure and true self that had done all that she could and simply needed to put herself " . . . into the hands of the giver of all good and perfect gifts . . . " (136-26) In spite of the daughter's efforts the elder woman died from her complications, but it become clear to the younger woman that she had done everything possible to help her mother.

The importance of wearing specific colors of clothing that would promote personal well-being or energize a specific vibration was often cited by the Cayce readings. Blue was frequently recommended as one of those colors. Throughout the readings the color blue was often cited as a source of healing, spirituality, vitality, life, and balanced development (physical, mental and spiritual). In regard to the rationale, Cayce told one individual, " . . . Blue, of course, brings the higher vibration to the entity." (2574-1) Another person was told that wearing blue apparel was a good idea as " . . . it will bring not only the vibrations of healing for the entity but a pleasant and a beautiful reaction to the mental efficiencies of the body." (2015-3) When one middle-aged woman inquired as to how she could overcome "vibrations that are not in attune with my own?" Cayce replied: "Filling self's mind (Mind the Builder) with those things that create more and more a unison of *creative* thinking, whether this be as applied to material, spiritual, or purely mental and social relations. Be sure they are *creative* in their essence." (303-2) Another individual was encouraged to wear blue because, according to the readings: " . . . *Blue* always worn about the body will create a vibration that enables the entity to think, as it were, without interruption; but the blue should be not dark—nor that real light—but more of an even shade . . . " (880-2)

As noted previously, individuals often have an affinity toward certain colors (as well as the appearance of certain colors in their aura) because of past lives and past-life experiences. As one example, the past-life influence of color was cited in a reading given to a forty-four-year-old entertainer who was told that in Rome she had once been in a position of authority and had also managed to emulate the qualities of justice and mercy. She could reawaken to the same energies of that experience, bringing a hopeful and helpful attitude to everyone she contacted in the present. In order to assist her in this regard Edgar Cayce recommended that she wear the color blue:

> Again we see *blue* as the color about the entity, or that worn next the body should ever be a portion of the dress. Not that as is of the mode (mauve), but rather that which stood in the Roman experience not for that flaunted in strength but as of power, of a might; yet tempered with mercy and justice. These are as innate, and find expressions in the mental body, in its visions, in its dreams, in its aspirations; while the material or the earthly sojourn may find the greater expression or manifestation in the senses of the body, in the glorifying of self's own abilities or activities. 729-1

The impact of color from a previous incarnation was also discussed in a reading given to a forty-two-year-old nurse. In her case the color blue was connected to a lifetime she had lived in Holland and was recommended for her vibration. In fact Cayce counseled that the color blue could help to reawaken her soul memories of that former period to such an extent that they would constitute *"proof"* for the individual of her previous lifetime. (114-1)

Elsewhere in the readings a forty-eight-year-old woman was told that one of her most important and relevant past incarnations was a lifetime in ancient Egypt in which she had been involved with ministry and healing. In order to reawaken the energy of that experience as well as the commitment and dedication that had been a part of her soul's purpose at the time, Cayce recommended that she wear fine linen clothing that was colored blue. (812-1) When another woman asked for advice in the care and raising of her eight-year-old daughter, the readings encouraged her to always give the child something blue to wear close to her body as an undergarment or as external attire, as it would have a beneficial vibratory influence upon the child. (608-7) Another woman was also encouraged to wear shades of blue with purple because of the high vibrations associated with those colors. (1554-4)

On one occasion the energy of blue was recommended for an eighteen-day-old infant. The reading suggested that blue (and mauve) could be an appeasing influence in the experience of this newborn, a child who would be extremely inquisitive and always want to know "why?" about everything. Cayce cautioned the parents that they would need to reason with their baby girl rather than simply demand things of the toddler. They were also encouraged to work frequently with their baby's capacity for imagination and visualization and—because of the child's temperament—"*never*" to let her wear red or even pink. (1775-1)

The reading given to a twenty-one-year-old housewife recommended that she always wear something blue and that she also always carry upon her person something that had been carved. In an effort to explain the rationale for each, the reading stated that these were both to serve as a "counterbalance" to urges and inclinations that would impact the woman in the present. These inclinations entailed distrust and intolerance, both of which she had acquired in a recent past life in France. Cayce explained, as follows: " . . . You will rarely find individuals being intolerant with others with something intrinsically carved being worn; or never very, very mad with blue being worn . . . " (578-2)

Almost as an afterthought a twenty-four-year-old woman in her eighth month of pregnancy asked about the color of her aura in the midst of a physical reading dealing with her pregnancy. (Note: one month later she would give birth to a healthy baby girl.) Because the woman had been giving a great deal of thought and preparation to her pregnancy (some of which was reflected in the questions she asked), Cayce stated that her present "developments and influences," especially connected to the mental and spiritual realms, had caused her aura to be mostly "blue to those of purple." He recommended these same colors for her, stating that they would be complimentary to her pregnancy and the child she was carrying. He also advised that she stay away from too much green, black, or deep red, as these colors would not be of the highest vibrations in terms of her present activities. (301-8)

The colors of purple and blue were also indicated in the aura of a fifty-five-year-old school board secretary who asked Edgar Cayce for a life reading. She sought career advice and guidance as to how she could begin to develop her own psychic abilities. When she asked for a description of her own aura, Cayce provided the following:

> *Auras are* twofold. That which indicates the physical emanations, and that which indicates the spiritual development. These when they are kept more in accord with the experience of individuals make for the greater unification or purpose and ideal.
>
> The aura, then, is the emanation that arises from the very vibratory influences of an individual entity, mentally, spiritually—especially of the spiritual forces.
>
> In this entity in the present there is signified a blue and a purple, or a bluish purple; indicating the spirituality, the spiritual seeking that has been as a portion of the entity's experience through the earth. And these may be magnified, not only for greater mental and spiritual development but for the maintaining of a better physical equilibrium. 319-2

Indigo and Violet

The shortest wavelengths of visible light are indigo and violet. Cayce noted the following in regard to these colors:

> Indigo and violet indicate seekers of all types, people who are searching for a cause or a religious experience. As these people get settled in their careers and in their beliefs, however, these colors usually settle back into deep blue. It seems that once the purpose is set in the right direction, blue is a natural emanation of the soul. Those who have purple are inclined to be overbearing, for here there is an infiltration of pink. Heart trouble and stomach trouble are rather common to persons with indigo, violet, and purple in their auras.
>
> Venus is the planet of indigo, and La is its musical note. The moon is the planet of violet and Ti is its musical note. In

> the early church, indigo and violet meant humiliation and sorrow. (See *Auras* booklet, Appendix I)

As noted previously while discussing the spiritual centers of the body, the colors of the three highest spiritual centers are blue (thyroid), indigo (pineal), and violet (pituitary). It is for this reason and the vibration of these higher colors that the meditation room at the international headquarters of Edgar Cayce's A.R.E. in Virginia Beach, Virginia, was furnished with a preponderance of blue, indigo, and violet. (EdgarCayce.org) Some visitors, conferees, and members of the organization's prayer group have commented over the years that simply by coming in contact with these colors there is an immediate feeling of attunement and relaxation.

Carol Ann recalls how the energy of a room can take on a dynamic of its own. On such an occasion she had the opportunity to watch Rev. Alex Holmes, a Presbyterian minister, speak to her Parapsychology and Medicine class for doctors and nurses: "The aura around him was filled with deeper green, violets, and medium to darker blues. The energy in the room where he was doing the healings was so strong it made me 'high.'"

The Cayce files note the energetic power of violet as it relates to clothing in the case of a three-year-old child whose grandmother had obtained a reading regarding the child's personal direction and past lives. During the course of that reading Cayce mentioned the enormous impact that the vibrations of purple and violet would have upon the little girl. He suggested that those colors would help to bring a balance among her developing physical, mental, and spiritual forces and improve the child's activities in her relationships with others. A few days later the grandmother had the opportunity to experiment with Cayce's recommended color. She was at a Study Group meeting when she explained her experience, which was written down by one of the group members and passed along to the Cayce archives:

> Grandmother [413], at a Group #1 meeting of A.R.E., was telling of experimenting with colors for the child, purple and violet for physical disorders as suggested in the life reading.

> The child had been fretful and cross and was displeased with her playmate and everything she did. The grandmother noticed this and thought of what the reading said. The only thing she could find in the house of purple was an old evening dress, with beads on it. This she brought out and hung it on the chandelier in the room in which the children played, with the excuse to let it hang there and air out.
>
> The playmate immediately stopped and exclaimed over it, how pretty it was, etc., reaching out and touching it. [324] objected at first but when the playmate admired it so, she stopped and reached out and touched it also, looking at it for a long time. Her crossness seemed to disappear and she [the grandmother] had no more trouble with [324] the rest of the day. 324-5, Report #1

Bright clothing colors such as the color purple were also recommended to a thirty-eight-year-old telephone operator because they possessed "better vibratory forces." (513-2) Another person was advised that mauve and violet would serve as healing colors to the individual. (3374-1)

The vibration associated with any and all shades of violet was recommended in the case of a forty-three-year-old woman suffering from anxiety, tension, and psychosomatic illness. The woman's fears (mostly associated with relationship issues) continued to wear down her physical body. Cayce recommended that she begin focusing her mind upon more positive influences such as Unity's *Daily Word*. She was also encouraged to use odors and fragrances to which she felt drawn, as they would help her to feel more relaxed. In addition to working with prayer and meditative concentration she was further counseled to surround herself with the color violet. In fact Cayce stated that violet possessed a very high vibration that the woman could give to others if she was able to overcome her fears and refocus her mind in a more healthy direction. (4286-1)

On another occasion a woman in her forties contacted Edgar Cayce for help with health problems that seemed related to toxemia and poor circulation. In terms of color, she was told that rather than being a positive influence, certain shades of green had such a negative vibrational impact upon her as to almost draw illness to her physical body. She was also told that her health issues were connected to her dissatisfaction with life. The woman would later comment that " . . . housework is 'killing' me." (428-8, Report #1) During the course of the reading she was encouraged to surround herself with colors such as "purples or violets." The reading stated that these colors would help bring her joy and enthusiasm and also enable her to accomplish much that has " . . . lain dormant in the abilities of the entity in the present experience . . . " (428-4) She was also encouraged to pursue both creativity and a sense of purposefulness in the field of art. She would later tell friends how her life had turned around because of the reading's advice and provided the following testimony:

> I suppose it is known to most of you here that I have always had a very strong leaning towards art, but outside of my husband no one encouraged my endeavors at expression. After I had nursed my mother through a period of illness, I was again completely exhausted. I had a reading made to find out, what the trouble was. One of my questions was: How I could strengthen my body in order to meet the demands that were made upon me and Mr. Cayce's answer was that if I directed my energies into the fields of art, I would feel as never before. Of course I had heard things like this any number of times, but never dreamed that it could apply to a housewife. The jump from the one into the other has not been easy, as anyone can imagine, but every time in these last three years, when I was hopelessly 'out', my strength quickly came back when I busied myself with paper and pencil and also every time when art work predominated any length of time. I felt years rolling off my back . . . 428-8, Report #1

In her own work, psychic Carol Ann Liaros has noticed the frequent occurrence of the colors violet and blue in the auras of individuals attending her workshops. Carol Ann stated, "I have noticed various shades of blue, from pale blue to a deeper blue in the auras of many individuals in my workshops over the years." Upon talking to these people Carol Ann has come to discover that the "newbies" (those individuals just starting to work with their intuition) exhibit paler shades of blue, whereas the more involved and committed students possess medium blues. Those who are active meditators have the darker, more potent shades of blue in their auras. She goes on to say, "I have noticed that people who attend a workshop and are really committed to their own personal and psychic development tend to have violet in their auras. Those with violet or purple are the ones who really hear and experience the deeper messages of what is being taught."

In terms of conscious aura descriptions related to the colors green, blue, indigo, and violet contained in the Cayce archives, what follows are a few selected excerpts:

> . . . In the last few days, though you have had a great deal of purple, which means spirituality; the desires, the hopes for better things, and yet oft shaded with doubts or fears. You are *sure*, but a little fearful at times that you're not able to "put it over." You also have a great deal of coral, a great deal of pink—coral *and* pink, and at times *very pink*. Then at times you smear it more with green than you do with white; which indicates your desire to help others irrespective of themselves. That's not God's way. He doesn't help one to do other than help himself. Don't forget that! 288-31, Report #18

And,

> *Mae Roberts {no case number}*: You have a great deal of the shades of blue, some violet, and a little pink. So you are very definite in what you think, and in the things you do. You know where you are going, or think you know.
>
> [1223]: Your aura changes very much at times, because it goes up and down. You have a great deal of blue, but a shade of blue in the lighter shades—which would indicate your sureness as you go along with your study and your development. It opens to activities that indicate blue, white

and gold. As long as you are sure you can go. When you are not sure, you stop.

[2533]: You have more violet in your aura than anyone in the room. Violet always indicates the seeker, the searcher for something. You have more of than gray, blue, opal, white or pink. A great deal of pink or coral in an individual's aura indicates material-mindedness. 5746-1, Report #2

5 The Meaning of Colors (White, Black, Gold, and All the Rest)

White

Every school youth knows that white light passed through a prism of glass produces a rainbow of colors: red, orange, yellow, green, blue, indigo, and violet. White is essentially the sum total of all color, combined together in balance. It is the color associated with wholeness as well as perfection and holiness. On one occasion a waking Cayce told an individual: " . . . white means purity, always." (5746–1, Report #2) Edgar Cayce's *Auras* booklet also confirms the uniqueness of white:

> The perfect color, of course, is white, and this is what we all are striving for. If our souls were in perfect balance, then all our color vibrations would blend and we would have an aura

> of pure white. Christ had this aura, and it is shown in many paintings of Him, particularly those which depict Him after the resurrection. You recall that He said at the tomb, "Touch me not for I am newly risen." He meant that as a warning, I think, for the vibrations of His being must at that time have been so powerful that anyone putting a hand on Him would have been killed—shocked as if by live wire.
>
> Color is light, and light is the manifestation of creation. Without light there would be no life, and no existence. Light, in fact, is the primary witness of creation. All around us there are colors which we cannot see, just as there are sounds we cannot hear, and thoughts we cannot apprehend. Our world of comprehension is very small. We can only see the few colors between red and violet. Beyond red on one side and violet on the other are unimaginable numbers of colors, some of them so bright and wonderful, no doubt, we would be stricken blind if by some chance we could see them.
>
> But in the fact of these colors we cannot see, these sounds we cannot hear, these thoughts we cannot apprehend, lies the hope of evolution and the promise of eternity. This is a small and narrow world, and beyond it are the glories which await our souls. But if we labor to expand our understanding and our consciousness, we can push back the limits a little bit even while here, and thus see a little more, understand a little more. (See *Auras* booklet, Appendix I)

While giving a reading and observing the Akashic records for a sixty-three-year-old writer, Cayce made the unusual statement that the record for the individual was "beautiful" and "all white." Later on in the reading the suggestion was given that the individual was to write as one of the main purposes for her lifetime. She was also encouraged to hold as her ideal "universal consciousness" and an application of "I Am My Brother's Keeper." In this way she would hold true to the purity of white that was apparently a part of her innate abilities. In the language of the readings: "For in such a manner may ye bring to self the constant springing anew in the hearts and souls of the *many*, that beauty, that whiteness, that cleansing which is exemplified in the lotus flower." (1837-1)

On another occasion when a forty-nine-year-old housewife asked about the meaning of the appearance of "white lightning" that she had apparently seen in a number of visions, Cayce told her it was indicative of the "awakening" that was coming into her consciousness. He went on to say:

> More and more as the white light comes to thee, more and more will there be the awakening. For as the lights are in the colors: In the green, healing; in the blue, trust; in the purple, strength; in the white, the light of the throne of mercy itself. Ye may never see these save ye have withheld judgment or shown mercy. 987-4

The mother and grandmother of an eight-year-old-girl were told that the child was extremely sensitive—sensitive to the point of being "supersensitive." That sensitivity might lead to her being judgmental or wanting to avoid people as easily as it might lead to her feeling misunderstood or inferior. In addition to providing a range of suggestions for child-rearing such as encouraging the young girl to take part in drama, advising that the parents raise her with love and firmness but never with anger or scolding, and recommending that the child be surrounded with opportunities for musical expression (especially piano), Cayce also suggested that the girl frequently wear the colors of white and blue in her apparel. It was also suggested that a white or blue stone as a necklace would be extremely helpful. The rationale indicated in the reading was as follows: " . . . This is the better form of vibration for the entity, keeping a temperament gentler and more open." (2683-1)

During a reading given to a thirty-five-year old man suffering from blindness and cataracts, after providing a suggested regimen of treatment, Cayce was asked what color would be beneficial to meditate upon to stimulate "self healing." The response was: "The white light of the Christ, if the body, in itself, would find help . . . " Cayce went on to say, " . . . It isn't the color, it isn't the vibration—it is rather the awareness of entering into the spirit of truth, the power of health, the power of love. Do that." (1861-11) Follow-up reports confirmed that the recommendations were followed and that Mr. [1861] had regained partial sight in one of his eyes—an amazing occurrence since [1861] had been blind from birth!

The colors most recommended to a fifty-one-year-old woman were white, purple, and mauve. The reading stated that these three colors were not only a portion of the woman's aura but that they would also be the best colors that she could include in her personal attire. The reading went on to explain that because of differing past lives the woman possessed opposing urges that could be moved in more positive directions with the use of these three colors. On a positive front, various past lives had left her with a love of things that were holy and a desire to attune both her spiritual and mental self to that which was of a spiritual nature. On the negative side she was prone to intense procrastination, a harsh temper, and excesses of a sexual nature. Her past lives indicated that she had been a member of the French Court as well as an ambassador and unifier of people and ideas in ancient Egypt. When she asked for a description of her aura and its significance, Cayce replied:

> . . . White and mauve and purple become, or are, the *natural* emanations or activities from emanations, that are ever better about the entity. Hence we find in the aura the physical and the mental and spiritual emanations, that show for developments and retardments as well as abilities for the studying, classifying and applying of same. However, as indicated, the entity oft is dilatory—or inclined to procrastinate. Rather then let it be up and doing while it may!
>
> 1612-1

Black

Black is associated with the unknown or the unconscious. It may also correspond to death, evil, that which is repressed, and that which is hidden from others. Although some individuals believe black to be the combination of all colors, the reverse is actually true. The color black is the absence of light and is therefore the absence of color. Most often black is not considered to be a positive or uplifting color. As a case in point Carol Ann Liaros recalls a story from her own experience while working with the Human Dimensions Institute:

> A prominent psychic from a foreign country was arriving to present a workshop at the college. Predisposed to liking and respecting this well-known man from what I had heard about him, I was shocked when he walked into the room to greet the circle of about twenty people who were there to welcome him. When I looked at him and saw his aura, there was black at the top of his head in the shape of a witch's hat! The rest of the aura was an unpleasant gray and pea green color. I was stunned.
>
> As he greeted the people in the circle he spoke for a minute or two to each one until he came to me. He shook my hand, said hello, and quickly moved on to the next person. His aura was extremely unpleasant and threatening and felt heavy and "sticky."
>
> Several years later when meeting with a parapsychological researcher who had worked with this same individual, I was told that this psychic had been involved in the Black Arts and was a sexual predator! No wonder the image of a witch's black hat had appeared in his aura.

Using the color black was advised against during a reading given to a manufacturer of health products who inquired about the advertising, packaging, and color scheme of various remedies. The reading suggested that individuals consciously or subconsciously associated each color with specific thoughts and ideas:

> . . . let's take it from their own color scheme. Do not use these: Yellow, nor black, nor red. Now, what have we? The blue package with the white lettering would, then, make a preferable type. For, as the psychology of a sales proposition: That which catches the eye the quicker, people will ask about—even if it is sitting on the shelf of a drug store! Yellow partakes of those things that are contagious. Red, of those

> things warned of or against. Black, that which is of death itself. Then, blue and white! 1800-20

Gold

Gold corresponds to that which is valuable and worthwhile and may even be associated with the Divine. It is also related to spiritual truths and personal attainment. Cayce stated that the highest color vibration was contained in the colors gold and purple. For this very reason a reading done in May 1930 recommended the colors purple and gold for Atlantic University. (2087–3)

Gold was one of the colors recommended to a twenty-five-year-old bookkeeper who sought several readings on health, career guidance, business advice, and pursuing her life's purpose. The woman's file in the Cayce archives states that she suffered from low self-worth and self-esteem, as shown according to the archival notes:

> . . . Throughout her childhood and adolescence she had suffered keenly from an inferiority complex because of her slight stature and her constantly ailing health. Her older sister, born ten months earlier than she, had the advantage not only of being of normal size, but also of being prettier and the pet of their widowed mother. 2448-1, Report #4

On her own the woman had complained about not being able to find "contentment" and not being "happy mentally." She inquired by what means she could find strength, support, happiness, contentment, as well as how to overcome the depression that was giving her the "desire to leave this body." In terms of her life's direction, the reading advised that she was especially gifted with a talent for helping others choose their apparel. With this in mind she was encouraged to work in the dress goods business, perhaps ultimately owning her own store. In fact Cayce provided her with the names of several dress shops in her area that she was encouraged to contact for employment. She was told to work with others for somewhere between a year to a year and a half to understand the business before opening her own. Cayce also suggested that when she opened her own shop the colors that would create the best vibration for her, her body, and the business she was trying to create would be gold and light blue. (2448–3) The Cayce files also contain a conscious reading of Ms. [2448]'s aura. The description of her aura occurred five months after obtaining her first reading:

> [2448]: Your aura might be called a crown entirely, with gold, purple and pink; because things must measure up materially as well as spiritually and mentally. It is very beautiful. Gold, of course, means that you have attained to some understandings in which you are very sure.
>
> 5746-1, Report #2

Demonstrating the connection between past lives and an individual's affinity toward certain colors is the case of a thirty-year-old secretary. She was told that a former life influenced her attraction towards royal colors associated with Persia (e.g.: gold, black, blue, and red). According to the reading, in a past life she had been the daughter of one of the Egyptian rulers. During that incarnation she eventually married and rose to the position of queen of Persia. The colors she felt so drawn to in the present were a holdover from that period and " . . . things having to do with rule . . . and customs in various places." (5125–1)

Gold was also cited as one of the predominant colors in the dream of a twenty-one-year-old woman who dreamed in part that she was with her mother or mother-in-law and was purchasing a dress. For some reason she noticed that she was wearing a gold headband that dressed her hair like a turban. The saleswoman told her the dress she has chosen was pretty, but her mother (or mother-in-law) told her it was unbecoming.

Cayce stated that the golden headband symbolized the new thoughts, ideas, and truths that were changing her understanding of life. The saleswoman was representative of those who understood that these new ideas were " . . . golden in its action to the mind and truth as seen . . . ," whereas the mother (or mother-in-law) symbolized individuals among her family and friends who would criticize and disagree with her pursuit of these new truths and her developing understanding. She was encouraged to gain the lesson and remain steadfast in her pursuit of new information. (136-15)

On another occasion a thirty-six-year-old housewife was encouraged to pursue her innate abilities with healing, especially through the use of color, tone, and vibration. When she inquired as to the ultimate vibrational colors of each of the following: the basic elements of physical reality, the personality, and the ego, Cayce's reading responded with gold, blue, and white, respectively. (2441-4)

Miscellaneous Colors

What follows are some selected comments from both the Edgar Cayce readings and the work of Carol Ann Liaros pertaining to a variety of miscellaneous colors.

The colors of coral, purple, and rose were especially recommended to a forty-four-year-old woman who possessed an extreme sensitivity to both odor and color. Although no specific information was provided or requested, apparently these colors were suggested as most conducive to color sensitivities or as most helpful in overcoming the individual's sensitivity. (1877-1)

Purple was also recommended to an eighteen-year-old girl who was encouraged to wear the lapis lazuli stone. Cayce stated that the young woman's aura was vibrationally in accord with purple because of her activities and her thoughts. She was advised to wear those colors that would have an affinity to her aura. In the language of the readings: " . . . Especially plaids, mauves, and certain colors or shades of purple are well; for they bring those vibrations that become in accordance with what may be said to be both the mental and the physical aura of the body . . . " (1532-1) Cayce told her that the color purple for her was synonymous with the personal spiritual development that was occurring in her life.

A sixty-year-old woman who spent much of her time going to classes and conferences was told that the colors gray and mauve (considered by some to be gray-purple) would help her to experience "harmonious emotions." She was encouraged to have those colors (or "delicate shades") as a part of her apparel at all times. (1847-1)

The readings suggested that gray could be one of those colors that pertained to depression or personal "dis-ease." While giving a reading to a forty-three-year-old probation officer Cayce affirmed that gray was one of the colors with which the individual most often had a vibrationally affinity. As a means of improving his own frame of mind and spiritual development, however, he was told that colors such as "yellow, orange and violet" would have a tremendous impact upon his own aura, as would the certain kinds of music such as the work of Franz Liszt. (478-1) In terms of a personal message, Mr. [478] was advised:

> Let thy going in, thine coming out, be in meekness of purpose serving the Lord. For unto him that is given much, much is required at his hand. "If ye love me," as He has given, "feed my lambs. Feed my sheep." For the service is unto thine brethren, and, "Inasmuch as ye do it unto the least of these, my little ones, ye do it unto me." 473-1

Carol Ann Liaros also cites an experience with the color gray:

> When my son was thirteen he was hospitalized. He contracted a staph infection while in the hospital and was put on a powerful antibiotic. One evening I arrived at the hospital about 11 p.m. to visit him. I found him asleep. Not wanting to wake him, I sat for a few minutes; and as I did, suddenly I was aware that his aura was gray—ranging from light gray to a medium gray! I was shocked as I knew this meant something was very wrong. I requested the doctor see me immediately.
>
> I tried to explain to him that something wasn't "right" with my son (who was now awake because of the commotion). The doctor suggested that it was because they had had a difficult time getting his latest needle in and my son had gotten upset. Knowing the doctor wasn't really listening to what I had to say and knowing I couldn't tell him how I "knew" something was wrong, I hurried home to call a doctor friend of mine who had privileges at the Children's Hospital.

> I explained what I saw and why I was concerned. The doctor told me to meet her at the hospital the next morning.
>
> When I arrived I received very distressing news. Although a blood count had been taken every day, somehow the doctor in charge had not been monitoring it closely because my son's white blood cell count was dangerously low. My son had to be put in reverse isolation across from the nurse's station, and everything and everyone admitted to his room had to be sterilized. I was also told that if he got an infection at that point, he would not survive!
>
> Needless to say I monitored his aura closely to make sure the gray was disappearing and his normal aura colors returned! Thankfully, he did improve and remains fine to this day.

The color brown is often associated with that which is grounded as well as that which is associated with business. Certainly that was the case in a reading given to a thirty-year-old bookkeeper who was told that she possessed much inner stability and sereneness as well as having attained the knowledge of that which was "practical in those things of the world." When she asked which colors she had the most affinity with, the first color cited for her was brown, followed by purple and mauve. (2390-1)

In her own work Carol Ann Liaros has also found a connection between brown in the aura and an individual's affinity to business:

> The auras of my business clients usually had a nice, steady-looking brown in the aura, which was also verified when I had the opportunity to work with executive vice presidents in the corporate world. Sometimes, however, I noticed that there was "too much brown" in the aura of some of the managers with whom we were working. I came to understand that too much brown suggested they were "stuck in the mud" and would not go as far as others in their careers. I learned a great deal about people and the meaning of colors from interpreting the appearance of auras in my readings.

The importance of all kinds of colors, "deep color," "pastel shades," and so forth was emphasized in a reading given to a fifty-three-year-old interior decorator. The reading suggested that the woman's affinity with color was traceable to a past life in ancient Egypt. At that time she had apparently excelled at understanding the influence and harmony of color as well as the spiritual significance of color in {*many*} individuals' lives. Those same abilities remained with her in the present. Cayce's reading advised her to continue her work in decorating (as well as in writing and speaking). Helping others would enable her to emphasize the importance of spirituality, color, and harmony in every individual's life, especially as those ideas could become understood in the decorating of people's homes. (1833-1)

A career in decorating or even jewelry design was also recommended in the case of a sixty-one-year-old naval employee who worked as a food inspector. The reading cited his abilities with color, especially as they related to the colors of various stones. This ability was such that Cayce counseled he could " . . . bring a great deal of joy, of harmony into the experience . . . " of anyone with whom he worked. Apparently he had an innate talent for understanding the color and vibrations of stones—especially emeralds, opals, and semi-precious stones. Cayce added: " . . . for each of these have their value in the effect, the vibrations that they bring . . . " He went on to suggest that a moonstone could promote the vibration of peace, harmony, and things of a spiritual nature. Bloodstone could help to reduce any tendencies of anger. The man was also encouraged to correlate the colors of stone with the colors in the human aura and was told that he would find a connection between the two ninety-nine percent of the time. (5294-1)

Stones were also recommended in a reading given to a twenty-four-year-old receptionist who was encouraged to wear pearls. In the language of the reading, "The pearl should be worn upon the body, or against the flesh of the body; for its vibrations are healing, as well as creative—because of the very irritation as produced same, as a defense in the mollusk that produced same." (951-4) Cayce told the same woman that anything of beauty—whether in nature, movement, the atmosphere, a painting, or a song—had a positive resounding vibration upon her. She was encouraged to often wear clothing that was colored royal blue, purple, or violet for the helpfulness of these particular colors to her own vibration.

A sixty-two-year-old artist was informed that her attraction to color was inextricably connected to her ability to experience the higher vibrations and even the "emotions" of color. Part of her artistic calling was—according to her reading—being moved by color " . . . finding the divine in color, harmony, in tone, in music—as if it were the voices of the spheres." (3706-2) Cayce added that her affinity with color was with all colors, especially in the form of pastels.

Parents of an eight-year-old girl were told that their daughter had experienced realms of consciousness (e.g., "inter-between" experiences in consciousness between lifetimes) that essentially entailed experiences with noble purposes, broad vision, and love. The "niceties" of these experiences in consciousness could become a larger influence in their daughter's life as she wore delicate shades—especially lavender, pink, and green. (665-1)

A sixty-one-year-old podiatrist was advised that the color purple and the odor of lavender would help her with attunement. (688-2)

Purple and lavender were also recommended for mental issues in the case of a twenty-two-year-old woman who had begun exhibiting signs of mental illness after her junior year at college. According to Cayce, the young woman's problems had occurred as a result of nerve strain breaking down her previous mental balance and harmony. In addition to a therapeutic regimen that included spinal adjustments, medicine, and keeping her mind focused on uplifting materials, Cayce recommended the following:

> Keep about the body the colors of purple and lavender, and all things bright; music that is of harmony—as of the Spring Song, the Blue Danube and that character of music, with either the stringed instruments or the organ. These are the vibrations that will set again near normalcy—yea, normalcy, mentally and physically, may be brought to this body, if these influences will be consistently kept about this body.
>
> 2712-1

Interestingly enough, the color purple was actually advised against in a reading given to a two-day-old girl. In analyzing the infant's emotional makeup Cayce stated that the baby would grow to be extremely temperamental and would always insist on having her own way for the first fourteen years of her life. Emphasizing the soul's ability to control others, he added that she would also " . . . wrap most of those about it {*her*} around itself {*herself*}, in one manner or another." She would also be prone to extremes—even swaying between having a very beautiful character to having a "very ugly" character. The reading suggested that the parents could work with this extremely bright and talented child by using patience and teaching through example. The reading also indicated that the girl would grow to have a very "strong physical body" and would be drawn to the influence of music.

The reading provided the parents with advice for child rearing and encouraged them to learn how to help their daughter express and work through her anger. Cayce counseled, "Never have things mauve about the body, nor much purple. Rather the blue and pink, delicate shades, and shades of white and green—these will make for a much more even temperament and bring environs of greater strength." (1958-1) According to follow-up reports on file:

> Mother reported she had all the problems indicated—every single prediction was absolutely true. She had her hands full with the child until she was in her teens, then the child leveled off, becoming quite grown up and no longer a problem. Quite early in her teens she became a dancing teacher, starting her own school; very independent and successful.
>
> Immediately after her eighteenth birthday she married a nice young man and started raising a family.
>
> 1958-1, Report #2

Occupational guidance occurred in the case of a thirteen-year-old girl who was told that she had the ability to minister to others through color. Cayce told her that colors possessed both an appealing influence and one that promoted harmony. Extremely in tune with color vibration she was told that she could become most helpful to individuals by assisting them in *"harmonizing"* tones, shades, and colors. (276-3)

Ironically during the course of a physical reading given to a forty-two-year-old woman who was suffering from stomach problems and allergies, Cayce told her that she was as allergic to color just as some people were allergic to pollen! Apparently the allergic reaction had developed in response to an ongoing misdiagnosis of her problem. She was encouraged to obtain physical adjustments to her spine, which would improve the overall vibrations of her body and eventually assist her in overcoming the problem. The woman followed the recommendation and found immediate improvement for both the stomach problems and the allergies. (5511-1)

Another instance of being allergic to color was cited in a reading given to a young boy. The boy's parents were told that in addition to pollen, their son's asthma and allergies were irritated by color. Apparently injuries to the spine as an infant along with a fall at the age of four had heightened the problems, which the readings described as a sympathetic and psychopathic condition. In this instance, Cayce also recommended spinal adjustments by an osteopath or chiropractor and told the parents that such adjustments would result in a permanent cure for their son. (5468-1)

Although not suggestive of an allergic reaction, an adult woman was told that her desire to wear "somber colors" was in direct opposition to her sympathetic nervous system. Apparently the woman's attraction to somber and dark colors was contributing to her worries, nervousness, and tension. Vibrant colors were more in keeping with the upbeat attitude that could facilitate overcoming her anxiety. (4119-1)

Conversely, parents of a two-year-old boy were encouraged to dress their son in the somber colors of nature, especially colors associated with the spring and autumn, as those colors were most in tune with the youth's vibration. Cayce further commented that the boy would give special notice to these specific colors. (1990-3) In an interesting note on file his aunt recalled the following incident when the boy was two and one-half years old: " . . . he spent a summer with his grandmother who made corduroy overalls for him. His mother always selected autumn colors for him—greens, blues, orange, etc. He would pick up the scraps from the floor and exclaim, 'Look, Grandma, aren't they beautiful?' . . . " (1990–3, Report #14)

A change in clothing was also recommended in a reading given to a thirty-one-year-old unemployed female who was advised to refrain from wearing "shades" of colors but instead to wear tints—especially, " . . . white for purity, the blue for purpose, {*and*} the red for the strength needed." (2378–1) She was also encouraged to wear a symbol of Queen Elizabeth I's coronet (rose crown?) out of sight, as its vibration would help to make her "invincible to men or to others!" On another occasion, Edgar Cayce consciously read the woman's aura, stating the following:

> [2378]: You have a very good aura. Most of yours is blue, with not white but a gray light. You are sometimes almost sure of yourself and then not sure at all. It doesn't take the shape of long points, or just a cloud, but more as a fold—which would be like a turban about your face and shoulders.
>
> 5746-1, Report #2

The readings suggest that there was a time in ancient Egypt when individuals were encouraged to choose colors for their attire that were "harmonizing" to the colors of their own aura. As one example, a twenty-seven-year-old lecturer and designer was told that "harmonizing" individuals to their unique aura was, in fact, her innate talent. A career in the field of color was recommended, especially as it related to the movies or cinema, as this media would provide her with the greatest avenue of outreach to the greatest number of people. In terms of outlining an appropriate means of furthering her education in the field of color, Cayce suggested the following:

> As for colors pertaining to life itself—as the self or the entity set in motion, *study* auras and aid *others* in knowing what they mean! There are those that interpret same in the form of spiritism. There are those that interpret same in the form of vibration. They are *all* of these and more, as the entity *knows* and may *experience!* 1436-2

According to notations on file rather than pursuing or finding success in cinema, a decade later the woman had written a book analyzing "color and personality," which was apparently well received. Years later she was a frequent lecturer on the topic of the psychology of color. (1436–4, Report #4)

6 Feeling Versus Seeing the Aura

*One of the most memorable experiences Carol Ann Liaros recalls con-*cerning "feeling" an individual's aura occurred while she was still working as a psychical research subject at Rosary Hill College in New York. She was standing at the receptionist's desk checking on her next appointment when, according to Carol Ann, "it felt as if a wall had crashed into me!" When she turned in shock to see what was happening she saw a nine-year-old boy standing about three feet away from her. The boy was with his father; the two of them were actually her next appointment. The father had requested a reading, looking for assistance with his autistic son. The rigidity of the boy's aura had slammed into Carol Ann like a brick wall. During the reading she discovered one of the child's major issues. Approximately every other word was able to penetrate his very rigid aura in order to actually reach his ears! Part of the boy's speech problem with repeating incomplete sentences happened because he was hearing incomplete sentences.

Although this appointment became one of her most memorable experiences with "feeling" the aura, it was far from the first. In fact Carol Ann Liaros admits that originally she did not "see" colors in her work with auras but instead "felt" the colors and the aura itself:

> In the beginning I felt the auras and the colors of the aura with my whole body and could describe the colors only from the feeling I was experiencing. Then I began to see more and more of the energy of the auras which then developed into seeing the colors with greater clarity. Sometimes it was a combination of seeing and feeling together.
>
> Afterwards for approximately ten years, my predominant experience was seeing the aura. That's when I was truly able to work with identifying and interpreting the colors. For the past few years I seem to be back in the mode of "feeling" the colors in the aura. I have yet to be able to identify why this ability—at least in my own experience—seems to change.

Carol Ann Liaros also remembers an experience with "feeling" auras when two identical-looking vitamins were placed one in each hand. Carol Ann recalls, "As I felt the aura energy from the vitamin in my left hand, it felt smooth and harmonious. However, the auric energy in my right hand felt jabbing and sporadic." The researcher working with her repeated the experience numerous times, each time giving her a vitamin for each hand; and each time Carol Ann described the fact that one felt "harmonious" and one felt "sporadic."

When the experiment was over the researcher explained that she had repeatedly placed a natural vitamin in one of Carol Ann's hands and a synthetic vitamin in the other, and on each occasion Carol Ann had described the natural vitamin as "harmonious" and the synthetic as "sporadic." Carol Ann was especially surprised by the result as she divulged, "At that time I had no interest in or knowledge of vitamins—synthetic or otherwise."

Another example that clearly illustrates "feeling" an aura is the story of a middle-aged businessman named Scott who was invited to a dinner with other corporate executives specializing in health care administration. Scott describes how he sat down at a table with several others including a very successful businessman—a Mr. Zheng from China—who spoke no English. Thankfully there was a translator and a bilingual doctor nearby who could assist Scott in his communication with the Chinese executive. Anxious to hear about the businessman's own experience with health care in China, Scott asked several questions and waited for the response to be translated. Scott describes what happened next, as follows:

> In spite of the fact that I don't speak a word of Chinese, while the individual was speaking I watched him as though listening to his every word. To my great surprise something started to happen as soon as he started speaking. It is hard to describe, but I somehow "felt" that this man had an *incredibly powerful* insecurity issue with his own father. The thought wasn't logical on several fronts: first of all, I didn't know this person; secondly, I had never "felt" how an insecurity issue in someone else might feel; and thirdly, this businessman was actually taller and huskier than I was. The fact that he could be insecure made absolutely no sense to me. Therefore, I ignored this very strong feeling and just continued to listen—first to the businessman and then to the translator.

After hearing the response Scott asked another question about the status of health care in China. As soon as the businessman started speaking Scott felt the "feeling" again, only this time more powerfully:

> It is hard to explain even now, but in addition to the overwhelming feeling that this man had an intense insecurity issue with his father, I heard the words, "This individual needs help in healing his relationship with his father." And the words repeated themselves.

Scott then describes how he was somehow "pushed" into mentioning this issue to the bilingual doctor: "I felt crazy, but I turned to the doctor sitting next to me and said, 'I get the feeling that Mr. Zheng has an issue with his father that he needs to work on.'" According to Scott:

> The doctor looked very surprised. A personal friend of Zheng's, he acknowledged that Zheng had been so challenged by his ongoing relationship with a father who did not or could not see his son's worldly success that Zheng had gone to counseling in the United States, as such a thing was not common in China.

Scott continued, "I felt like the experience had happened to me for a reason, so later in the evening I spoke with Zheng (through the translator) about my own experience with insecurity and how I overcame it. In the end I think Zheng was grateful that we had had the opportunity to sit together that evening. Truly, 'feeling' this man's energy was an amazing and memorable experience."

In terms of the Edgar Cayce information, while giving a reading to a fifty-eight-year-old jeweler in 1944, Cayce recommended that this individual begin working with more of his own innate psychic abilities. These abilities, Cayce suggested, occurred for the individual whenever he became cognizant of his feelings within the beauty of nature: " . . . the spirit of a rainfall, a sunset, a river, a tree, a herd, a flock, a school of fish—from these the entity may gain, as in the aura from same, much that to others would be imagination . . . " (3657-1) In fact, Cayce suggested that in his most recent incarnation he had been a writer who was very adept at descriptions. Apparently his ability to feel the vibration and aura surrounding all things was so developed that he could evoke a sense of those same feelings in others through his writing.

On another occasion in the Cayce files, a fifteen-year-old student who was interested in psychic ability asked about his own budding intuition and whether or not he had learned to read auras correctly. Cayce's response was, "Not always . . . " (361-4) The reading went on to suggest that there was both a physical and a spiritual component to auras—one was apparently a visible manifestation of the individual's thoughts, activities, health, and so forth. The other component was essentially vibratory in nature and emanated from the level of the soul—providing insights into past lives as well as soul growth, development, and shortcomings. Cayce suggested that the young man's intuitive exercises had enabled him to attain the ability of seeing the physical component of auras. It was clear that he needed to work harder to perceive the spiritual component. The young man was encouraged to work with prayer and meditation and to begin noticing what vibrations emanated from himself after doing so. With practice he would learn to subject his physical perception and rely more upon the "feelings" of another person's aura. Prayer and meditation would deepen his attunement to the spiritual ingredient of auras.

Certainly, Carol Ann Liaros's work with the blind has demonstrated countless times that individuals can just as easily be taught to "feel" an aura as they can be taught to "see" an aura. In actuality the training is the same. For many years Project Blind Awareness excelled as an innovative training program for blind participants, enabling them to become more mobile and independent through the use of their intuition. Founded by Carol Ann Liaros, the program received ongoing media attention and even became the subject of prime time television during one of the episodes of *That's Incredible*, which aired in the 1980s. During the episode Lisa Hoffman, a fourteen-year-old blind student with glass eyes, demonstrated how Project Blind Awareness had enhanced her intuition through the technique of "mind traveling," also known as "remote viewing." The purpose of this technique from the perspective of blind participants was to enable visually handicapped individuals to become familiar with strange surroundings. Using their intuition helped to decrease their fear of new places and assist them in becoming more mobile and independent.

The episode of *That's Incredible* filmed Lisa Hoffman lying in a horizontal position at her family home in Rochester, New York, while Carol Ann Liaros stood near her to lead the fourteen-year-old girl through the imaginary mind travel or remote viewing experience. The episode turned out to be the film crew's first experience of documenting a "live" parapsychological event. Just prior to filming, Carol Ann was handed a slip of paper with a California address written on it. She instructed Lisa to imagine that the young girl was "flying" to the address—a private home where no one in the room had ever been, including the film crew.

As Lisa approached the front door of that address in her imagination, she pretended to reach out and touch it. Her description included the fact that it was made of wood and had a small window that contained an even smaller wood carving within the window. When the *That's Incredible* episode aired on television, another film crew had shot footage of the actual house. As Lisa was describing what she was "seeing," the television audience saw a stained wood door with a small four-inch-by-four-inch window and a red-painted wood carving within the small window.

Following Carol Ann's instructions, Lisa pretended to enter the doorway and was told to notice what was on her left, her right, and what was straight ahead. Lisa stated that she could see three doorways that led to three different rooms, including the living room to her immediate right. (While this was occurring, the television audience was shown that there were, in fact, three doorways leading to various rooms, including the living room to the right.) As she stood in the doorway of the living room, she commented that it was light, bright, and airy—also true.

Carol Ann next suggested that Lisa imagine that she was entering the living room and was told to find where the couch was located. The fourteen-year-old described two couches facing one another. She stated that she could see many handmade pillows on them with an unusual table between the couches. Lisa said that there were candles and books on the table, and she added that both couches were beige. (In reality, two couches were facing one another, and there was an unusual table in between that was essentially a cross section of an enormous tree trunk that had been shellacked. However, one couch was beige and the other was blue. There were handmade pillows on the couches that had been made by the mother of the woman who lived in the house. The television audience also saw that there were two candles and several books on the unique table.)

Lisa was next asked to touch the walls and to notice what was hanging in the windows. Carol Ann gave this instruction thinking there might be paintings or pictures on the walls and blinds or curtains in the windows. After hearing the instruction, Lisa pretended to run her hand over the wall. She described it as being rough-textured and said that she noticed something cold and hard hanging in the window. At this point, she used her hands to indicate the shape of a crescent moon. (The film crew had shot the actual walls that were rough-textured stucco and a neon light in the shape of a crescent moon hanging in the window—the exact shape Lisa had made with her hands.) Lisa went on to communicate the number of windows and chairs that were in the room. Although she was correct with the number of chairs, at first it appeared that she might have overstated the number of windows by one. However, as the film crew demonstrated, there was another window covered by a standing screen. Interestingly enough, it was a window that would not have been apparent even to a sighted person who actually might have been standing in the room.

When Lisa was asked to "pay attention" to anything else that caught her awareness, she said that she could "see" a piece of furniture being used as a bookcase. (In reality there was an antique desk in the living room that the owners were using as a bookcase rather than a desk.) She was asked if there was a fireplace anywhere in the room. She responded that the two couches faced the fireplace. In addition to describing fire irons she seemed delighted to find that "there are several art pieces of metal welded together." (In reality there was a fireplace with fire irons, but above the fireplace on staggered shelves were art pieces of metal welded together. It turned out that the father of the woman who owned the house was an artist whose medium was welding pieces of metal.) Finally Lisa described a clock on the mantel and used her hands to show the shape of the clock.

According to Carol Ann Liaros, "It was stunning to watch her hands follow the exact form of the clock. Another interesting aspect of this show was the fact that when the film crew left Rochester no one had any idea whether she was wrong, right, or partially correct. It was a surprise and even a shock when the show finally aired, and we were able to see just how correct Lisa had been in her 'imagination.'"

Another individual who demonstrated adept abilities with a heightened sense perception in spite of being blind was a Jesuit priest, Father Schommer, then artist-in-residence at Canisius College in Buffalo, New York. (See also the Chapter Three discussion regarding "yellow.") Father

Schommer described his experience with Project Blind Awareness to Carol Ann Liaros as one in which he came to understand that "blindness brought light." Schommer admits that in the beginning blindness "struck at the very roots of my identity." Thankfully the program enabled him to "see" the world in a different way, enabling him to become receptive to a heightened state of awareness in which the feelings, emotions, and vibrations of the outside world could somehow be accessed. According to Schommer, "color does have a sensation" that can be felt. Schommer admits that the sensation of color originally perplexed his rational left brain and his years of higher education. He describes his personal experience with heightened intuitive perception, as follows:

> First, it has opened up a cosmos to me who thought, after becoming blind, that I was cut off from the world which I loved and cherished . . . [It has also] made the distinction that cerebral accuracy is quite different from sense accuracy and I am comfortable in these terms with this realization . . . I could [also] say that in my case, life has just begun at sixty due to Blind Awareness . . . One relaxes into the reality of his own being with which he has been so familiar for many years and comes out a far wiser, a more mature, and far more responsive and understanding person.

From her work with Father Schommer and from witnessing his ability to "feel" the frequency of energy, Carol Ann Liaros developed a technique that she called "aura scanning" that she has used with both sighted and non-sighted students. She describes one use of the technique, as follows:

> First, I ask participants to pair off with a partner. To begin, one partner holds his or her hands a few inches from the other individual's body and scans the aura around his or her partner to experience width, density, and so forth. After this auric scan takes place, I ask the one being scanned to begin doing mathematical calculations in her or his head: addition, subtraction, multiplication.

> Meanwhile the partner doing the scanning would again scan the aura around the head. Inevitably the one doing the scanning will find the aura fuller and more active on the left side. Conversely, if I ask the partner being scanned to pray or meditate during the experience, the one doing the scanning will find the aura fuller and more active on the right side. It is an amazing experience.

Another use of aura scanning is to have each partner scan the other's aura to find any physical changes (e.g.: temperature fluctuations, weaknesses, surgeries) or difficulties, and then to have the partners reverse roles. From Carol Ann's experience, this is one technique in which the blind have truly excelled over the sighted. Perhaps the best explanation is that the sighted may be visually distracted, while the blind can only pay attention to what they are able to feel or sense. This same technique of "aura scanning" can be used to scan the auric colors as well as the activity levels and health of the chakras.

Working with an object such as a light bulb is another technique that Carol Ann has used with both the blind and the sighted to enable participants to "feel" energy. Once again individuals are told to choose a partner, and each group of partners is given a light bulb. With closed eyes, the one doing the scanning first traces the outline of the light bulb. After tracing the outline several times, the individual then imagines "feeling" the aura emanating from the light bulb.

Next, the partner doing the scanning is asked to hold the light bulb up to the middle of her or his forehead (the "third eye"), pressing it lightly against that area. He or she then moves the light bulb several inches from the forehead and again "feels" the aura of the light bulb. Each partner is given the opportunity to feel the energy of the light bulb.

Afterwards one of the partners is asked to take the light bulb and hold it several feet out from his or her forehead. The other partner is asked (with eyes blind or closed) to imagine expanding the personal aura to touch the aura of the light bulb and trace it with her or his own energy. The same experience is repeated with the other partner holding a different object (such as a square piece of dice or a round marble), and the partner expanding her or his aura is asked to identify the object by expanding the aura and attempting to "feel" what kind of an object the partner is holding. According to Carol Ann, "The success with this technique has been astounding. I've even asked participants to do this experience with the object being held by the partner behind the head, and it works just as well!"

Additional publicity for Project Blind Awareness resulted from a landmark publication, *Super-Learning* (Ostrander, Ostrander, and Schroeder), which documented the experience of Father Schommer and other blind participants who were able to "feel" and "see" things that were far beyond the perception of most sighted individuals:

> They kept practicing relaxation, visualizing the bio-fields of energy around the body, sensing colors . . . As they came to realize that even their limitations might not be as real as they thought, these blind men and women started to do things that they all readily admit "sound incredible."
>
> Some started to recognize colors far across the room. The world began coming back into "sight" in a way they found very hard to express—they were connected again, but in a new way. There seemed to be a light in their heads, some said, where before there had been only darkness. One man retired his white cane, for he was somehow aware of lamp posts, jutting storefronts, steps, and curbs. A completely blind woman "saw" a photograph . . . As relaxation and training continued, these solid citizens started learning how to travel in their minds' eyes to distant rooms, houses, offices—places they'd never been to—yet they were able to describe the layout. In ESP lingo, theirs is clairvoyance pure and simple. Yet it's hard to square these people with the usual "psychic" image. They never thought of themselves that way either.[6]

---

[6]Sheila Ostrander, Nancy Ostrander, and Lynn Schroeder, *Super-Learning* (New York: Dell, 1979), 220–21.

According to *Super-Learning* all of the Project Blind Awareness sessions were documented with written, taped, and photographic records. Principal researchers included Dr. Douglas Dean, an electrochemist and parapsychologist at the New Jersey Institute of Technology, and Dr. Sean Zieler, a clinical psychologist at Veterans Hospital in Buffalo, New York, and an advisor in the study. Before training in blind awareness, participants were documented as being able to pick out colors (green versus red) or black and white at a level corresponding to chance. After training in relaxation, visualization, sensitivity, and aura scanning, participants were tested again. As noted by Dr. Zieler, "The more they did it, the better they performed—sixty-five to seventy percent accuracy, with some getting a perfect score." He went on to add, "Some of the things that happened were mind-boggling."

Another participant in Project Blind Awareness was Lola Reppenhagen, whom Carol Ann labeled as "one of our star pupils." Lola worked with relaxation every night and practiced with the Project Blind Awareness color cards (attempting to discern the color of each) every day for fifteen minutes. At first red seemed to be the most visible color for her. She noted it, for example, on a book that was lying on her counter, and confirmed with her husband that it was red. The more she practiced the more frequently colors came to her, often during "unexpected" times. Lola documented her experience to Carol Ann, as follows:

> I find it difficult to believe the things that are happening. I have not yet learned to tell each color every time and some not as well as others, but it is coming. I've had some success with mind travel. My awareness of my energy field is developing. I feel as though I can see my hands working, I see my body, I see images and shadows and seem to be able to almost see what is in a room. It seems that I really see it, although I don't, I am totally blind.

Another Project Blind Awareness participant named Barbara, a school teacher in her mid-twenties, was very bitter about becoming blind. She attended each of the sessions and was becoming frustrated that "none of the training" seemed to be working for her. One week, however, she came to class very excited and eager to share her experience. According to Barbara she was startled awake in the middle of the night. She awoke thinking that her apartment was on fire since all of her furniture was glowing with a golden white light. Knowing that she couldn't "see," she felt for how much heat was emanating from the fire but there wasn't any. She turned to see "whether the light switch was on" but quickly remembered that she was completely blind. When asked what she did next, she replied: "I sat there and enjoyed seeing for about half an hour for the first time in over three years."

All of these experiences with the blind are truly amazing.

It is interesting to note a dream that Carol Ann Liaros recalls, beginning when she was around the age of twelve. It was a recurring dream that happened perhaps several times a year, right up until the time that she began working with Project Blind Awareness. The dream seemed to predict her involvement with the blind:

> I was standing in the doorway of what I knew was a hospital . . . and the room was absolutely enormous with these huge high ceilings. I was standing in the doorway with what I thought were two doctors. We were "floating" across the room, not walking, and I began to observe that there weren't any beds in the room. There were people standing all around, sort of aimlessly. While we floated past these people, they would look over their shoulders toward us with a strange look on their faces. What shocked me so was the look in their eyes. It was an absolutely tortured look. I knew as we were passing them that we were healing them, but we weren't doing anything.

Looking back, Carol Ann realizes there were no beds in the "hospital" because the people weren't really sick, and their eyes were tortured because they were blind. She believes the dream symbolizes her work with helping the blind to see. After more than forty years of training individuals to see auras and work with their own intuition Carol Ann knows with certainty that "You don't have to be sighted to *see* an aura and you don't have to be blind to *feel* an aura." Anyone can be taught to experience the aura, whether it is feeling the vibrations, literally seeing the aura, understanding the significance of energy emanation, or also in time learning to comprehend the meaning of colors. Experiencing the aura is something that is available to everyone—it is just a matter of training, practice, and perception.

7 Experiencing the Aura for Yourself

Even if you've never seen or believed it was possible to see an aura you can learn how to see auras for yourself. Just as your eyes are able to look at your hand placed in front of your face and then refocus on the wall on the other side of the room, you can teach yourself to see the energy that surrounds everything. Rather than staring at something or squinting, the ability to see auras is really a technique of soft, passive, and receptive seeing. It is retraining yourself to look at things and people differently as well as learning how to refocus your attention and your sight. Requiring practice, it is simply learning how to do something new.

As an analogy, do you remember when you were a child learning to ride a two-wheeler? You probably had training wheels on the bicycle and a parent alongside of you on a smooth pavement, setting up the ideal conditions for you to learn. Once you had the feel of the balance, however, there was no longer any need for those "ideal conditions" for you to be able to take off and ride freely. Seeing auras is a very similar experience. At first you might need guidance and training, as well as the ideal conditions for you to be able to see the aura. You might want conditions such as appropriate lighting, black or white clothing being worn by the person whose aura you are trying to see, or having a black or white background or screen for the person to stand against, and so forth. In time, however, you will be able to see auras without guidance or assistance and even when conditions are not ideal.

If you tend to be a visual person, learning to see auras might be easier for you than it would be for a person who is more auditory or someone else who is more kinesthetic. Conversely it might be easiest for a kinesthetic person to *feel* the aura than it would be for an individual who is more visual or another who is more auditory.

Perhaps some of the questions that arise when discussing the ability to see auras are, "Why is seeing auras worthwhile?" or "What are some of the practical applications of seeing auras?" The possible answers to these questions are nearly limitless and include the following:

- Becoming cognizant and aware of another's mood
- Being able to "scan" your child (or someone else) for physical, mental, and emotional health
- Being able to discern whether or not someone is telling the truth
- Seeing depression (or other emotional issues) in an individual and being able to respond to that person with kindness
- Assisting those who are having conflict
- As a teacher, speaker or presenter, being able to see if students or participants are "getting it"
- Attuning to a colleague's aura before beginning work
- As a medical professional, being able to diagnose physical problems
- Understanding another's position on a specific issue by seeing or experiencing the situation the way the other individual does
- The list continues

Actually most individuals are "sensitive" to auras, energy, and personal vibration; but most of us are not culturally predisposed to understand this dynamic of our personal psychic sense. Edgar Cayce believed, however, that everyone had some familiarity with auras and vibrations even though they might not realize it:

> "But what do auras mean to the majority of people, who cannot see them?" you ask? Well the majority of people do see them, I believe, but do not realize it. I believe anyone can figure out what another person's aura is in a general way, if he will take note of the colors which a person habitually uses in the matter of clothing and decoration. How many times have you said of a woman, "Why does she wear that color? It does not suit her at all." How many times have you said, "How beautiful she looks in that dress. The color is just right for her. She was made to wear it." In both cases you have been reading an aura. The first woman was wearing a color which clashed with her aura. The second woman was wearing a color which harmonized with her aura. All of you know what colors are helpful to your friends and bring out the best in them. They are the colors that beat with the same vibrations as the aura, and thus strengthen and heighten it. By watching closely you can even discover changes in your friends as they are reflected in a shift in the color predominating in their wardrobe. (See *Auras* booklet, Appendix I)

Because they have not been taught otherwise, children are generally one of the easiest groups to be guided through the visualization of the colors and energy of an aura. As one example, Carol Ann Liaros recalls the story or her son Dean, who was in a special class for dyslexia with six other boys. One day when her son was nine, he told her that his class had just learned about Helen Keller. He went on to say, "I told the teacher that my mom teaches the blind to see with the third eye . . . She wants you to come and speak to our class about the work you do with the blind." Although wondering what the teacher truly thought about her work, Carol Ann agreed to a date. She describes the day of the experience, as follows:

I knew the attention span of a nine-year-old to be approximately a minute-and-a-half, and I was expecting Dean's entire dyslexia class of six or seven children. To my surprise word had gotten out to the entire school about my appearance. My presentation was scheduled for the auditorium, which was literally filled with nine, ten, and eleven-year-olds and their teachers.

To begin I started talking a little bit about the energy that radiates from all of us, and how it has different colors and is of different widths. I explained that it tells things about us and our personalities and can tell us things that are physically wrong with us. I stood in front of the school's white movie screen and asked to have the lights dimmed. I had them close their eyes and take a deep breath for a little relaxation. I then stated, "When you open your eyes, open them just halfway and look at the energy radiating from my body; and tell me what it looks like."

The children weren't at all self-conscious about answering. One of the children shouted that she could see blue; someone else saw yellow. A number of others confirmed the same colors.

I next told the students, "You can feel the energy too," and I had them imagine that they could feel the aura of the person sitting next to them. Everyone had a good experience and seemed to be enjoying the exercise.

However, leave it to an adult to change all that. One of the teachers stood and asked, "How do we know you haven't just hypnotized them? You've told them it's got energy and it has colors. Is there any scientific research to prove this?"

Of course, the children didn't care about that; they all saw and felt the auras. Sighing inwardly, I asked aloud if there was any teacher present who had something wrong that was physically hidden. One of the teachers stepped up in front of the screen, and I asked the children to follow the same procedure—close their eyes, take a deep breath, and relax. When they opened their eyes halfway, I instructed them to

> look at the aura carefully to see if they saw anything different at any place on the body. Once again they all saw the energy similar to that around a lighted match, and some saw colors. All of a sudden many students in the group shouted out that they could see dark gray around the teacher's hands and wrists. Interestingly enough the teacher was wearing a long-sleeved shirtwaist dress.
>
> I asked her to tell us about her physical problem. She stated that she had gone skiing over the weekend. While she was skiing she had lost her balance and caught her fall using both hands, resulting in two sprained wrists. Her choice to wear the long sleeved dress was to hide the bruising on her arms.

For some people, there can be stumbling blocks when they start trying to see the aura. One of the major stumbling blocks for many individuals is their own intellect. The person may begin to see a color, a shade, or some aspect of the aura, only to have his or her mind undermine the experience by saying something like, "Yes, but it's probably just the lighting in here, it's my imagination, or I'm just following the suggestion and believing what I am told to see."

Another stumbling block is past conditioning. We've been taught to believe that it's just nonsense; that there is no such thing as an aura. Or perhaps some of us have been conditioned to believe that seeing auras is a specialized skill that can only be done by great psychics or individuals who are very spiritually evolved. That belief is not true. Although it is true that individuals who have worked with their spiritual growth, meditation, and raising their own consciousness might have an easier time seeing auras, vibrations, and the subtleties of various colors, anyone can do it.

Probably the best approach to overcoming these obstacles is practice. With practice not only will you be able to experience the fact that auras surround all things and all people at all times, but you will also be able to discern some of the differences contained within each and every aura—differences that can be verified by the individuals whose aura you are seeing. For example, practice seeing the auras around healthy people, and then look at the auras surrounding people who have a physical problem of some kind. In time you will be able to see how that problem appears in the human aura. You can also practice on yourself, in front of your own mirror.

Another obstacle for some people is that they may see "something," but they are convinced that an aura has to look a certain way. They fail to realize that the something they are seeing is actually one of the ways in which the aura can manifest to human perception. The following example is drawn from the Edgar Cayce files:

During a follow-up reading given to Ms. [275], a twenty-one-year-old woman interested in numerous topics contained in the Cayce material, she inquired as to why a friend of her father's had seen a blue light between Mr. Cayce and herself during a particular reading. The man had been present for reading number 5750-1, in which a group of individuals had asked Edgar Cayce to discuss " . . . an historical treatise on the origin and development of the Mayan civilization . . . " The man, (a Mr. MacBeth), described what he had seen as simply a blue light that seemed to exist between Mr. Cayce and Ms. [275], connecting them in some way. During her own reading, the young woman asked what the light meant.

Cayce stated that the blue light had essentially emanated from her as a sympathetic blue aura. Apparently during the time of the reading she had been so focused on what Mr. Cayce was doing and was so inclined to assist him if she could, that the blue light had manifested in her aura as a means of "conjunction or coordinating or cooperating" with that which was occurring. (275-37) In other words her intent was to be helpful in any way she could, and her vibrational energy field had connected to that intent, providing the sleeping Cayce with energy that could assist him during the reading's process. Mr. MacBeth had seen an aspect of the woman's aura—the blue light that seemed to connect her with Edgar Cayce. In other words, he had seen the aura without realizing that was what he was seeing.

The time has come for you to practice seeing the aura. Let's start with something non-human, like a plant.

PRACTICING SEEING THE AURA

Practice session with a plant

Sit somewhere where you are comfortable: close to a plant, shrub, or tree. You may choose to sit indoors or outdoors. When you are comfortable and have the plant nearby, relax and take a deep breath. Breathe in relaxation and breathe out any tension. Breathe slowly and deeply, noticing how your breath feels cool as you breathe in and warm as you breathe out. Relax again and breathe.

While breathing and relaxing, turn your attention to the plant or greenery near you. Send love and appreciation to that plant. Feel the energy that you are sending out to that plant. Imagine that the energy is surrounding and embracing the plant. While feeling and imagining the energy, adjust your eyes (perhaps by squinting, refocusing, or looking more gently). Now begin to become conscious of the energy field around this plant. Try to see and feel the aura of this living thing. You may see a faded outline, some bands of energy, and perhaps some color. Focus on the plant and become aware of what you are seeing or feeling.

As soon as you start to see the aura of the plant certain thoughts may occur. Your intellect might tell you that it is only your imagination. You might begin to believe that your eyes are playing tricks on you—you might think that you're seeing a shadow, a reflection, or that it's only an optical illusion. Sometimes, people wonder whether or not they should get their eyes checked. These are very common responses.

While you're observing the aura begin to notice what happens to the aura around the plant as you send the plant love and appreciation. You may see the auric field expand, grow, and become more luminous in response to the energy and appreciation it is receiving from you. Take the time to look at every area of the aura surrounding the plant. Gaze upon the entire outline, and when you are finished send out a "thank you" for this energy exchange. Take another deep breath and re-ground yourself in the present.

Alternatives to this exercise may also include looking at the aura and exchanging energy with a family pet or feeling the energy of an inanimate object.

Sometimes individuals ask for further clarification on what some of the "ideal conditions" might be that can best enable a person to see and experience an aura for him or herself. If you are just beginning to work with auras the ideal conditions might include taking the time for a relaxation exercise, making certain that you are seated in a comfortable chair, using a white (or black) background behind the person or object you are looking at, and taking the time to adjust a room's lighting so that it is more advantageous for you. For example it may also be a good idea to have very soft lighting such as working in a room with a dimmer switch, or perhaps working in a room during the day with the lights off so that the space is semi-dark.

After relaxing and getting centered half open your eyes so that you can maintain an unblinking, peripheral vision. Look to the side of the person, plant, or object for which you are trying to see the aura. Relax into that area of focus. Don't look directly at the individual, plant, or object; instead, look at the outline which surrounds your test item. That is where the aura is; it radiates out from the individual or object. Try to use your sight with soft, passive seeing. It is not staring; instead it might best be described as a passive, gentle, soft looking. Generally your eyes will be partially open—perhaps only half open.

At first you might see an intensification of the color behind the object or individual—perhaps a glow, similar to the energy around a lighted match. The energy that you'll begin to perceive may look like waves of motion, an extended outline, a haze, or a cloud. It may be brighter surrounding the object, or it may contain intense color. Frequently as individuals begin to see auras, they may simply see a hue of white; others may see what looks like an intensification of color behind the person or object.

Sometimes as soon as an individual begins to see an aura he or she can get very excited and blink, causing the aura to give the impression of disappearing. Rather than thinking, "It went away," the aura didn't actually go anywhere. The aura is constantly present. As individuals blink the eyes refocus back to their normal way of "seeing" the physical world. To see the aura again all the individual needs to do is look at the aura again with the passive, gentle approach to seeing this higher, finer level of energy.

In time and with practice you will begin to understand what it feels like to become relaxed, to open yourself up to heightened sensitivity, and to refocus your eyes. One of the best tools, of course, is practice. With more and more practice you will find that you can see auras even when the conditions are not ideal and even when you are not consciously trying to see them.

PRACTICING SEEING THE AURA

Practice session with self (including description of "relaxation exercise")

Teaching yourself to relax is one of the most important components of seeing the aura. One version of a relaxation exercise follows:

Get comfortable sitting in a chair or lying upon a bed or a couch. Next tense up your toes as tightly as you can. Make them as tense and as tight as possible. Now relax them. Then relax them even more.

Move your awareness to the muscles in the lower part of your legs; pay attention to the process that your muscles go through as you tense them. Tense the muscles in the lower part of your legs. Hold that tension. Relax. Now relax even more.

Next tense the muscles in the upper part of your legs. Make them tense and taut. This is what your body feels like when it's in a state of tension. Relax those muscles. Now communicate to those muscles to relax even more.

Proceeding to the muscles in your abdomen and lower back, make those muscles just as tense and as taut as possible. Then relax those muscles. Now relax those muscles even more.

Tighten the muscles in the upper part of your torso by hunching up your shoulders. Tense the muscles in your back and chest. Smoothly and gently relax those muscles. Communicate to those muscles to relax even more.

Tighten the muscles in both arms by clenching both fists: tense and taut; and then relax. Now relax even more.

Tighten all the muscles in your face, particularly around the eye area. We carry a lot of tension around our eyes, and then we wonder why we get headaches. Relax those muscles. Now relax them even more.

Let your head come forward and very slowly and very, very gently, begin to rotate your head in a big, wide circle. Rotate your head—first in one direction all the way around and then in the other direction—to relax the muscles in the neck and the upper shoulder area.

Finally tense every muscle in your body. Begin at your toes, working up your legs, through your abdomen and back. Hunch your back and shoulders, clench your fists, and make them tense and taut. Finish with your shoulders, neck, and head. Then very slowly, as if in slow motion, relax every muscle in your body. Slowly and smoothly, relax every muscle in your body. Tell those muscles to let go. Communicate to every cell and every muscle in your entire body to relax even more.

You are now in a state of relaxation.

This relaxation process is certainly an effective one to try for your practice. In the future you may wish to use additional relaxation and centering approaches.

There are many ways to begin to observe auras. One of the things anyone can practice is to look at his or her own aura. After you have relaxed you can try to look at your aura in a mirror. A smaller step might be to observe the aura around your hand.

After you have completed a relaxation exercise while lying in bed at night or during the day in a semi-dark room, turn your attention to the middle of your forehead as if you were looking at the middle of your forehead from the inside to the outside. Keeping your attention centered on the middle of your forehead is a very simple and very effective concentration technique. This technique is also said to stimulate the third eye—our ability to see psychically—and in this case to see auras. Whenever you feel your attention wandering, bring it back again and again until it remains in place as you continue to concentrate inside the middle of your forehead.

When you are ready take your hand and hold it in front of you, a foot or so away from you. Refocus your eyes (with the gentle, passive seeing). Try seeing the higher, finer level of energy that surrounds your hand. If you have trouble seeing it, move the hand closer or farther away until you get the sense of the energy field that surrounds the outline of your hand. Alternatively spread your fingers apart. With your eyes half closed observe the energy radiating from your fingers. You may notice immediately that it is relatively easy to see the aura surrounding your hand.

While continuing to breathe and relax, turn your attention to your arm. Attempt to feel the energy that is emanating from your arm. As you become receptive to the energy use passive seeing to look for the outline, light, or color that surrounds your arm. Adjust your eyes (perhaps by squinting halfway, refocusing, or looking more gently) and become conscious of the aura and any subtleties of energy. Focus again on your arm, and become aware of what you are seeing or feeling.

Begin to notice what happens to the aura around your arm as you send your body appreciation for all that it does for you. You may see the auric field expand, grow, and become more luminous in response to the energy and appreciation it is receiving from you. Send out a "thank you" for this energy exchange, take another deep breath, and reground yourself in the present.

After seeing the aura around your hand or arm you might want to use this exercise to try to observe in a full-length mirror the aura around your entire body. Alternatives to this exercise include trying to hold certain emotions or thoughts in mind while looking at your aura in the mirror. For example, you might send thoughts of love or healing to someone you truly care about—a child, a grandchild, a spouse—while looking at your aura. For contrast you might want to look at your aura while thinking something entirely different, such as, "I am so mad about ______________________________."

The purpose for this approach is to watch what happens to your aura as you think and feel warm, loving thoughts followed by cold, selfish thoughts. Maintain a playful, lighthearted feeling as if you were playing a game. If you try too hard nothing will happen.

PRACTICING SEEING THE AURA
Practice session with others

Ideally, practicing with a friend or practicing in a group with a number of people whom you don't know very well is a great way to begin seeing the aura of someone else. When you are working with another person, decide who is going to look at whose aura first, and who will go second. For this activity, wearing white or black, working in a semi-dark room, and taking part in a relaxation exercise will help with your experience. After relaxing, have the person whose aura is going to be viewed stand against the wall or a screen.

With half-open eyes look at the outline of the person. Don't look at the person and don't look at the wall; instead look where the energy is radiating from the person. Look all around the person's head, and his or her shoulders. Continue to look in a soft, unblinking way with your peripheral vision. Don't try too hard. Relax into the experience. As you begin to see the energy—whether it is a glow, an intensification of color behind the person, a haze, or smoke—whatever it is, say it out loud. Even if you think it's your imagination, say it out loud. If you see color, where do you see the color? Notice how wide the aura looks to you; see the vitality in the aura. If you wear glasses, try doing the exercises with your glasses on and then without your glasses.

If you are working with more than one person and two of you are attempting to see an individual's aura, the perceptions of each person should be verbalized aloud. If you say that you see "green" and the other individual states that she can see "yellow," ask her where she is looking. You may find that one of you was looking around the head and the other was looking somewhere else. Each aspect of the aura may have different colors in it. These colors are made up of who we are physically, mentally, emotionally, and spiritually. Take time to visualize the aura surrounding the entire person, and verbalize what you see.

When you have a general perception of the whole aura, look for where the aura appears different. Is there a place where the aura looks darker or where it is surrounded with the color gray? Is there a bulge or a break somewhere in the aura? Does it look as though it is lacking energy? Where does the aura look different to you? Is there something physically wrong with this person? Again, say anything that you can see out loud.

Change places when you've finished looking at the individual's aura. Give the other person the opportunity to see your aura and verbalize what he or she can see.

Once you've had the opportunity to look at the auras of two or three different people, you will begin to get a visual sense of how everyone is energetically different. Auras look different—some are wider, brighter, narrower, or harder to see. Some are more vibrant and colorful. Others are much weaker.

It is a good idea to look at the aura of someone who says that he or she has a physical problem—especially if you can't see what that problem is. Even a problem such as a headache, a neck ache, a backache, or a recent operation will have visible evidence in the aura. If you think you see something and you say it aloud, e.g., "I think you have a back problem;" and you end up being wrong, don't worry. It is a learning experience.

If you don't have someone at home or a friend with whom to practice, it is still possible to practice. One of the best ways is to pick a boring article from a newspaper. Alternatively, choose a lecture or a sermon in which you are not interested. With the news article, lecture, or sermon, try to follow intellectually what the speaker is saying. Soon the intellect becomes so tired that it zones out, and the right side of the brain overtakes the left side. Your eyes will change focus and you'll notice that you can see the haze, the glow, or the intensification of color of whatever it is that you're viewing.

Another way to practice is attempting to see the aura of someone with whom you are having a telephone conversation. Try to visualize the aura while you are speaking with the individual. Where does her or his aura radiate the most energy? What are the colors you can see? Is there an area where the aura appears to be smaller, as though something is not functioning properly? The bottom line is that there are many ways to practice seeing someone else's aura, even by yourself.

PRACTICING SCANNING THE AURA[7]

Practice session with others

In addition to visualizing the aura, scanning the aura is a great way

[7]Adapted from *Intuition Made Easy* by Carol Ann Liaros (Scottsdale, Arizona: Cloudbank Creations, Inc., 2003).

to tune into another individual. You will need a partner for this exercise.

After taking yourself through a relaxation exercise of some kind, stand facing your partner. Stand with your feet spread slightly apart and with your arms hanging at your sides. (Note: this exercise can also be done with both partners sitting, or with the partner being scanned lying on a table.)

As you face your partner, begin to get a sense of your partner's energy field by bringing the flattened palm and fingers of your hand slowly within approximately two feet of your partner's head. It is probably best to use your dominant hand. Slowly, move your hand closer to your partner's head until you can begin to feel the energy field emanating from her or his body. At no time will your hand actually touch your partner; you are solely scanning your partner's aura.

Once you can feel the outer edges of the energy field, slowly begin scanning the entire outline of your partner's aura. You are going to scan the area from the head all the way down to the toes. Beginning at the top of the head, scan the sides of the head, the back of the head, and then your partner's face. Next, scan under the chin and across the throat and neck area. One at a time, ask your partner to raise each arm to his or her side; and then scan along the top of the arm from the shoulder to the hand.

Work carefully over the hand, scanning each finger separately. Next, you will move your hand along the underside of the arm, beginning at the tips of the fingers to the armpit. Repeat this sequence for both arms.

Afterwards have your partner lift both arms as you scan across the torso from side to side. Scan the front of each leg, one at a time, from the hip to the foot. Scan around the toes. Then have your partner turn around so that you can scan the back of each leg from the buttock to the heel. Finally, scan across the entire back from side to side.

While you are scanning your partner's aura, try to maintain a relaxed and focused state of mind. Throughout this exercise your objective is to find any area in the aura that feels different. When you come to an area that feels somehow different, you may ask yourself, "What am I feeling, and where am I feeling it?" Then listen inwardly as you move your hand back and forth over the area until you are quite clear of the source. Communicate your feelings to your partner.

(Note for the individual being scanned: if your partner tells you of an area in the aura that feels different, think carefully before responding. Your partner could be picking up on an area from the past that is no longer an issue or perhaps a temporary condition about which you have yet to become aware.)

If you find that you are distracted by watching your hand or by looking at your partner as you scan the aura, try either closing your eyes or picking a spot upon the floor as a focal point for your eyes.

During this exercise, relax and try to have fun. The more relaxed you can be during this exercise, the better will be your results.

Trade places with your partner when you have finished the aura scan. After you have both had the opportunity to practice the exercise, take the time to once again share your experience with one another.

In her own work, Carol Ann Liaros has amassed decades of experience training individuals to see auras in a group setting. Some of her class ideas include the following:

> When instructing students in my classes, first I spend some time with different people up at the screen so the class can see that everyone's aura is different. We are different physically, mentally, emotionally, and spiritually; and we also have different past experiences, including past lives.
>
> Next, I try a few experiments. One is to have the students look at my aura. Then unknown to them, I try to manifest selfish feelings by saying to myself, "This is MY Ring, you can't have it. It's MINE!" I feel a selfish feeling as I say these sentences to myself. Inevitably, everyone will see the aura get smaller and darker! Then I relax, begin to meditate, and send love to them. Usually, individuals will yell, "Wow! It's getting bigger and bigger and brighter and brighter!"
>
> When showing the participants how to see auras, once instructions are given and we've gotten to the point where they can see my aura, I step several feet aside. There are gasps: "Your aura is still there!" Unlike the simple afterimage

> that is experienced when watching TV and looking away to see the negative of the screen, the auric energy left behind a golden glow. We leave the energy of our auras as well as DNA wherever we are. Perhaps this phenomenon explains the success of psychometry readings. Perhaps not, though, since photographs can also be read psychically.
>
> In a basic Intuition and Psychic Development class, I have everyone experience feeling auras, aura scanning, and seeing auras. To advance the class's experience of seeing auras, I will ask a student who has a headache to come up to the projection screen. The group is instructed to look at the overall aura for width, color, and brightness. Next, the group is asked to look at the head area and notice where the aura looks "different." Everyone speaks aloud where the darkness, bulge, or break in the aura is seen. We then find out from the student that the area corresponds to the location of the headache.
>
> At this point, I place my hands on the individual's headache area and perform a healing while instructing everyone to watch the aura. People are amazed as they see my aura and the subject's aura merging and the aura becoming larger and brighter. After a minute or two, I will take my hands away. The area usually is brighter and more energized. Even though it was a short period of time, the student reports that the headache is gone.

For more advanced work, try focusing on the overall intent of your practice session; e.g.: "My intent is to see any physical problems or areas of weakness," "My intent is to see and work with relationship issues," "My intent is to focus on the area of work and career," and so forth. The intent will connect you to that level of the auric field. You will find it both exciting and fascinating!

Ultimately, the most helpful tool when working with auras is to keep practicing.

Conclusion

*Color and vibration are all about us. They permeate everything that sur-*rounds us and all that we can see. Both are associated with energy as well as the ability to elicit particular feelings. Everyone has had the experience of having an affinity to particular colors or an occasion when he or she feels drawn to a particular color.

To be sure, there is a spectrum of color visible to the human eye; but there are also colors above and below the human spectrum that are not generally visible to human sight. In the same way there is a world of energy, vibration, and motion that surrounds all of us, even if most of us choose not to look. In fact, in spite of appearances we are not merely physical bodies but are instead spiritual beings made up of energy. As energetic beings we are connected to color and vibration in ways that we have yet to fully comprehend. Beginning to see auras can be a major step in understanding who we truly are.

Over the years the work of talented, intuitive individuals has repeatedly demonstrated that there is a world of activity beyond the sight of most people. It is a world that is just as real as the physical world appears to our perception. Psychic Carol Ann Liaros describes her work with auras, as follows:

> My experiences indicate to me that the aura contains the energy frequency of our state of health, which is comprised physically, mentally, emotionally, and spiritually. It also contains the frequency of our past, present, and future experiences, including past lives. Our conscious decisions are a frequency in the aura. With *intent,* one can connect to a particular frequency. I believe that the parasympathetic nervous system and the chakra system translate these frequency experiences into seeing (clairvoyance), hearing (clairaudience), feeling (clairsentience), smelling, and tasting psychically.
>
> Imagine a live TV show happening in the studio. The camera picks up the video; and it is transmitted through the air in a frequency form to your TV components, where it is transformed into pictures and sound. Likewise, all of your information is "stored" in your aura in a frequency form rather than in whole pictures. This transfer of energy from one to another is how the psychic information appears to me.

Carol Ann goes on to suggest that although the aura appears to radiate several feet from the body, her work over the years has convinced her that the physical body and its health are actually the end product of the aura. In other words, the vibrational energy we constantly emanate manifests eventually in the physical, including our own bodies.

The importance of auras was acknowledged decades ago by Edgar Cayce, the most documented psychic of all times. In hundreds of readings given over many decades, the Edgar Cayce information repeatedly expressed that each individual vibrated best to specific colors. That affinity was often connected to the individual's aura, and it was also connected to the traits, talents, and purposes a person was trying to create in his or her own life. Summarizing his lifelong work with auras and colors, Cayce had the following to say:

> Five hundred years before the birth of Christ, Pythagoras, the first philosopher, used colors for healing. Today medical science is just beginning to see the possibilities in this method. If colors are vibrations of spiritual forces, they should be able to help in healing our deepest and most subtle maladies. Together with music, which is a kindred spiritual force, they form a great hope for therapy of the future.
>
> But I do not think that color therapy will become widespread or practical until we have accepted the truth of auras and become accustomed to reading them in order to discover what imbalance is disturbing a person. Of course, we cannot transform all auras into a pure white light, but we can learn to detect signs of physical, mental and nervous disorders, and treat them in a proper way.
>
> An aura is an effect, not a cause. Every atom, every molecule, every group of atoms and molecules—however simple or complex, however large or small—tells the story of itself, its pattern, its purpose, through the vibrations which emanate from it. Colors are the perceptions of these vibrations by the human eye. As the souls of individuals travel through the realms of being, they shift and change their patterns as they use or abuse the opportunities presented to them. Thus at any time, in any world, a soul will give off through vibrations the story of itself and the condition in which it now exists. If another consciousness can apprehend those vibrations, and understand them, it will know the state of its fellow being, the plight he is in, or the progress he has made.
>
> So, when I see an aura, I see the individual as he or she is, though the details are missing. I believe the details are there, but they are missing from my perception and understanding. By experience I have learned to tell a good deal from the intensity of the colors, their distribution, and the

positions they occupy. The aura emanates from the whole body, but usually it is most heavy and most easily seen around the shoulders and head, probably because of the many glandular and nervous centers located in those parts of the body. The dark shades generally denote more application, more will power, more spirit. The basic color changes as the person develops or retards, but the lighter shades and the pastels blend and shift more rapidly as the temperament expresses itself. The mind, builder of the soul, is the essential governing factor in the aura; but food, environment, and other conditions have their effect. Sometimes outside forces bring about a change. I once met a man in whose aura I saw a shaft of light, coming downward over his left shoulder. In it there was some white, a great deal of green, and a great deal of red with blue mixed in it. I read this as a sign that the man was receiving information inspirationally, which he was using for constructive purposes. I wondered if he was a writer, for it struck me that this would be a proper aura for such work. I asked him, and he told me that although he had been a writer, he was now engaged in lecturing and teaching, still giving information for the help of others.

The shape of the aura is sometimes helpful. In children, for instance, it is possible to tell whether a great deal of training by example will be needed, or whether precept will do as well. If the child is reasonable and will accept instruction on this basis, the aura will be like a rolling crown. If example is needed, the aura will be a more definite figure, with sharp points and a variety of colors. If the child intends to be a law unto him- or herself, the aura will be like a rolling chain, lower than the position of a crown, going about the shoulders as well as the head. In the green aura of healers, if the color quivers as it rises, the person is most sympathetic. Several times I have seen people in whose auras there were little hooks of light here and there. In each case the individual had a job as overseer of large groups of others—a director and a leader. (See *Auras* booklet, Appendix I)

As the work of Edgar Cayce, Carol Ann Liaros, and others have confirmed, individuals can be taught to work with their intuition in order to see auras for themselves. In fact, there is a complex interaction between consciousness and psychic perception so that individuals can learn to perceive higher states of reality through personal training as well as through their own growth in personal consciousness.

The auric energy is also called "prana" by those in the East and "life force" by others. Obviously the more vital a person is, the more energy there is that can be observed in the aura. The healthier an individual is physically, mentally, emotionally, and spiritually, the wider his or her aura will appear. For those who are healthy, the aura is also brighter, has more vitality, and is easier to see. Individuals who are psychics, healers, or people who are seriously working with their spiritual growth have auras that might be described as "sparkly"—some describe it as the "sparkly stuff" that you may associate with fairy dust and the Disney movies.

The colors and shape of the aura have meaning to those who can see. If you have a person who is working on spiritual development, there is generally a lot of blue in the aura. If someone is depressed or ill in some fashion, there tends to be gray. Our moods, our thoughts, and our experiences are all reflected in the energy of the aura. Whenever there has been a physical change or a problem in the body, there will be a corresponding change in the aura. If you broke a bone when you were five years old, an x-ray will show that hairline fracture, and it will also be evident in your aura. Whether it is a healed broken bone, a health problem, or a heart condition, all of these qualities will be evident in the aura. The aura will also indicate temporary conditions such as indigestion from something you might have had for lunch or apprehension about a decision that you must make within the next week or so.

With practice it is very possible to learn to see and feel this energy that emanates from all things. It is an energy with both vibration and color that surrounds all that exists. For some, the aura might appear as energy, vibration, or feeling. Others describe how the aura consists of colors that provide visual information about the person, plant, living thing, or object from which the aura is emanating. Ultimately, the human aura is an energetic representation of the sum total of each and every individual. The aura gives off the story of itself. It is essentially a barometer of everything that is occurring, has occurred, or may be in the process of occurring in life. It provides information about individuals' physical, mental, emotional, and spiritual health, as well as about their experiences, relationships, strengths, and weaknesses. The aura contains the totality of the individual and is in a constant flow of potential change—altering and transforming based upon the thoughts, activities, and interactions with which each person is involved.

Appendix I Auras: An Essay on the Meaning of Colors—
the only booklet written by Edgar Cayce (ca. 1944)
Preface by Thomas Sugrue

NOTE: *Thomas Sugrue, author of* There is a River, *the original biography of Edgar Cayce, was the victim of a rare paralytic disease, and was saved from complete immobility and almost certain death by Mr. Cayce's "readings" for him. This preface, written less than two weeks after Edgar Cayce's death, reveals the deep personal and spiritual bond between the two men.*

The essay herein contained is the last labor to which Edgar Cayce put his hand. The color chart was returned to me with corrections in his own hand awkwardly written. With it was a note, also written in long hand. "I cannot use my typewriter," it said. "I have lost the use of my left arm and my right leg is numb. I presume I have had a slight stroke."

That was in September. A month before, on my porch here in Clearwater, while we watched the porpoises sporting in the Gulf of Mexico and admired the spectacular sunsets, the booklet was planned. The human aura was one of our favorite subjects of conversation; whenever we got together I questioned him about his ability to see colors emanating from persons, and he always had some new and interesting anecdotes concerning this strange power, which because it functioned while he was fully conscious, in many, many ways intrigued him more than his gift for giving readings. At least it entertained him more at the moment it was taking place, for despite all the readings he gave, he never heard one. During all of the most interesting portions of his life, he was asleep.

We were in the process of working out a new publication program during this visit, and it occurred to me that a short but instructive article on auras would be helpful to members of the A.R.E. {*Edgar Cayce's A.R.E.; www.EdgarCayce.org*} particularly if it carried Mr. Cayce's interpretation of the colors, worked out over a long period of years by patient trial and error. I made the suggestion to him, and he give me the usual answer—that he didn't know enough about the subject, had no background in it, etc., ad infinitum. He had a very low opinion of anything he said while awake. I then put it differently. I asked him if he would collaborate with me, and since he apparently had not the power to refuse me anything I asked (any more than he had the power to refuse anyone else), he said yes.

We set to work immediately, right there on the porch, and I began making notes. By the time the text was ready, he had returned to Virginia Beach, had fallen ill, and was at Roanoke resting. Early in December he was brought home to the house on Arctic Crescent. There, on the night of January 3, 1945, he passed away.

I remember him from those August days for so many things. He was so thin and tired and wistful. Yet his face lighted with transcendent joy when he saw me enter the water and slosh away on my own, swimming on my back in the warm, still water. He loved the Australian pines in front of our cottage, and wanted to have some sent to Virginia Beach, to plant along the lake behind the house. He was disappointed when he learned that they would not flourish that far north.

"Then I will have to come down here," he said. "You find a place, and we will get it together. I can rest here. I dreamed the other night that I was on a train coming to Florida. I had retired, and was going to live here."

I urged him to remain longer with me; I pressed him to give up the interminable, punishing hours he put in at the mounting stacks of correspondence. I suggested that he spend his time fishing and gardening, except for the periods when the readings were given. But those requests were to him unreasonable. In the letters which came to him were tales of misfortune and suffering. Each was a cry for help. He would have heard it as well in the garden or on the dock. If he could have answered it at once, he would not have minded so much. But when he had to put off the reading—at first for weeks, then for months, then for a year or more—his heart was heavy and his mind became numb with the burden of his helplessness. Though he stayed asleep longer than ever before and pushed his output of readings to unprecedented heights, he could make but a small dent in the pile of requests. It was this more than anything which broke him.

On the day he left, we drove with him as far as Lakeland. Along the way we stopped and ate a picnic lunch. Together we rehearsed our plans: publication and research were gradually to work their way to the fore of the A.R.E.'s work, giving to everyone the wisdom and instruction of the readings.

Gradually he was to slacken his own work until it was devoted mainly to general readings on research subjects and for guidance and instruction. In this way, the best that he had to give would be available to all. That way he would live long and help everyone, we were sure.

At Lakeland he stepped from the car and turned to smile at me and squeeze my hand. "Well, when we meet again we'll have everything worked out fine," he said. October was the date we had set. He would return then for a longer rest.

But the dreams that came to him here in our sunshine, and the whispers he heard in the Australian pines, were promises from another land. He will rest there, and just as he said, when we meet again we'll have everything worked out fine.

Two days after his death, the proofs of this booklet arrived. In them is his final message, a plea for faith, hope and charity, and above all, the courage and wisdom to engage in what Stephen MacKenna describes as, "an active mental life, with a little love to warm it." For the burden of all the readings is the necessity for man to take up his cross—"Mind is the builder: knowledge not lived becomes sin; in every person of whatever station look not for things to criticize, but for something you adore in your Creator; for you will not enter the kingdom of heaven, except leaning upon the arm of someone you have helped."

Thomas Sugrue
Clearwater Beach, Florida
January 15, 1945

AURAS
An Essay on the Meaning of Colors

Ever since I can remember I have seen colors in connection with people. I do not remember a time when the human beings I encountered did not register on my retina with blues and greens and reds gently pouring from their heads and shoulders. It was a long time before I realized that other people did not see these colors; it was a long time before I heard the word "aura," and learned to apply it to this phenomenon which to me was commonplace. I do not ever think of people except in connection with their auras; I see them change in my friends and loved ones as time goes by—sickness, dejection, love, fulfillment—these are all reflected in the aura, and for me the aura is the weathervane of the soul. It shows which way the winds of destiny are blowing.

Many people are able to see auras; many have had experiences similar to mine—not knowing for many years that it was something unique. One of my friends, a lady, who is a member of the A.R.E. told me this:

> All during my childhood I saw colors in connection with people, but did not realize that it was uncommon. One day the appearance of a woman in our neighborhood struck me as odd, though I could not for the moment see anything strange about her. When I got home it suddenly struck me that she had no colors about her. Within a few weeks this woman died. That was my first experience with what I have learned to look upon as a natural action of nature.
>
> Apparently the aura reflects the vibrations of the soul. When a person is marked for death the soul begins to withdraw and the aura naturally fades. At the end there is only a slim connection and the break is easy. I have heard that when people died suddenly, in accidents, the passing was very difficult because the way had not been prepared.

A person's aura tells a great deal about him or her, and when I understood that few people saw it and that it had a spiritual significance,

I began to study the colors with an idea of discovering their meaning. Over a period of years I have built up a system which from time to time I have checked with other persons who see auras. It is interesting to note that, in almost all interpretations, these other people and I agree. We only differ with regard to the colors which are in our own auras. This is curious, for it shows how universal are nature's laws.

We know that opposites attract and likes repel. Well, I have a lot of blue in my aura and my interpretation of this color does not always jibe with that of a person whose aura does not contain it and who therefore interprets it objectively. One lady I know has a great deal of green in her aura, and she is inclined to dislike green in the aura of others, and place a disagreeable interpretation on it, whereas it is the color of healing and a fine one to have.

Occasionally I have found, in books devoted to occult sciences, definitions of colors, and these are generally in accord with what I have found by experience to be true. The reading of any particular aura, however, is a skill that is gained over a long period of time by constant observation and endless trial and error. The intermingling of the colors, their relationship one to another, and the dominance of one over the other, are matters which must be considered before rendering a judgment. I am generally better able to "read" persons I know than strangers, although certain general characteristics of the strangers strike me immediately. But to be helpful I find it best to know the individual. Then I can tell him when I see the twinkling lights of success and achievement, or warn him when melancholy or illness threaten. Of course I do not do this professionally. I would not think of such a thing. But I believe it is an ability which all people will someday possess, and therefore I want to do what I can to get folks used to the idea of auras, so that they will think in terms of auras, so they will begin to attempt to see themselves.

I have been told that with proper equipment, it is possible for almost anyone to see an aura. Equipment has been built for this purpose, and I once met a professor who said that he not only had seen auras, but in his laboratory had measured and weighed them.

Where do the colors come from, and what makes them shift and change? Well, color seems to be a characteristic of the vibration of matter, and our souls seem to reflect it in this three-dimensional world through atomic patterns. We are patterns, and we project colors, which are there to those who can see them.

In his remarkable book, *Pain, Sex, and Time: A New Outlook on Evolution and the Future of Man*, Gerald Heard {*1889-1971*}, speaking of the evidence for the evolution of consciousness, points out that our ability to see colors is expanding. The easiest color to see, as you know, is red. At that end of the spectrum the waves of light are long. At the other end, where blue runs into indigo and violet, the waves are short. According to Heard, who is a reliable scholar, our ability to see blue is very recent. Natives who live on the Blue Nile in Africa do not know it by that name. Their title for it, when translated, means brown. Homer, all through the Iliad and Odyssey, describes the Mediterranean as the "wine-dark sea." Mr. Heard says that apparently Homer caught "the slight tinge of red in the purple of the Mediterranean," but did not see its predominant blue. Aristotle, moreover, said that the rainbow had only three colors: red, yellow and green. We all know that perspective in painting is recent, and it is apparently undeveloped in many primitive people to this day. I have heard, for example, that travelers in the remote Pacific Islands have found that natives looking at motion pictures are unable to perceive anything but a flat surface—their eyes cannot give three-dimensionality to the pictures.

So it would seem that our eyes gradually are gaining in power. I have heard many people comment on the prevalence of glasses {*or contacts*} among our civilized people. They have seemed to consider this a bad thing. Could it be that it is a result of constant straining on the part of our eyes to see more and to bring us to the next step of evolution? I think this is true and will be recognized in the future. What will it mean to us if we make this next evolutionary step? Well, it will mean that we can see auras. What will this mean? I am going to answer that by telling two experiences of a friend of mine who is able to see auras. This person, a woman, told me this:

> Whenever a person, whether it be a stranger, an intimate friend, or a member of my family, decides to tell me an untruth, or to evade a direct and frank answer to a question

> of mine, I see a streak of lemony green shoot through his aura, horizontally, just over his head. I call it gas-light green, and I have never known it to fail as an indication of evasion or falsification. I was a school teacher for many years, and my students marveled at my ability to catch them in any detour from the truth.

Imagine what that will mean—everyone able to see when you plan to tell them a lie, even a little white one. We will all have to be frank, for there will no longer be such a thing as deceit!

Now let me tell you the other incident that this woman described:

> One day in a large city I entered a department store to do some shopping. I was on the sixth floor and rang for the elevator. While I was waiting for it I noticed some bright red sweaters, and thought I would like to look at them. However, I had signaled for the elevator, and when it came I stepped forward to enter it. It was almost filled with people, but suddenly I was repelled. The interior of the car, although well-lighted, seemed dark to me. Something was wrong. Before I could analyze my action I said, "Go ahead," to the operator, and stepped back. I went over to look at the sweaters, and then I realized what had made me uneasy. The people in the elevator had no auras. While I was examining the sweaters, which had attracted me by their bright red hues—the color of vigor and energy—the elevator cable snapped, the car fell to the basement, and all of the occupants were killed.

You see what the knack of seeing auras will mean when it becomes a common ability. Danger, catastrophe, accidents, death will not come unannounced. We will see them on their way as did the prophets of old; and as the prophets of old we will recognize and welcome our own death, understanding its true significance.

It is difficult to project ourselves into such a world, a world where people will see each other's faults and virtues, their weaknesses and strengths, their sickness, their misfortunes, their coming success. We will see ourselves as others see us and we will be an entirely different type of person, for how many of our vices will persist when all of them are known to everyone?

One more comment on the possibilities of the future; then we will return to the more mundane present. Another person who sees auras once told me this:

> If I am talking to a person and he makes a statement of opinion which reflects a prejudice gained in one of his former lives, I see as he speaks a figure in his aura, which is a reflection of the personality he was in that time—I see, that is, the body of a Greek, or an Egyptian, or whatever he happened to be. As soon as we pass on to another subject and the opinion gained in that incarnation passes, the figure disappears. Later he will express another view. Perhaps he will say, "I have always loved Italy and wanted to go there," and as he speaks I will see the figure of a Renaissance man or an old Roman. During the course of an afternoon's conversation I may see six or eight of these figures.

Well, what is that but a Life Reading, except for the interpretations and judgments? It sounded so strange when I heard it that I was inclined to be skeptical, until one evening at dusk when, sitting on the porch of a friend's house, I saw the thing myself. My friend was speaking earnestly to a group of people and he made some interpretation of English history. In his aura I saw the figure of a young monk, and I recalled that in his Life Reading this friend had been identified as a monk in England.

"But what do auras mean to the majority of people, who cannot see them?" you ask? Well the majority of people do see them, I believe, but do not realize it. I believe anyone can figure out what another person's aura is in a general way, if he will take note of the colors which a person habitually uses in the matter of clothing and decoration. How many times have you said of a woman, "Why does she wear that color? It does not suit her at all." How many times have you said, "How beautiful she looks in that dress. The color is just right for her. She was made to wear it." In both cases you have been reading an aura. The first woman was wearing a color which clashed with her aura. The second woman was wearing a color which harmonized with her aura. All of you know what colors are helpful to your friends and bring out the best in them. They are the colors that beat with the same vibrations as the aura, and thus strengthen and heighten it. By watching closely you can even discover changes in your friends as they are reflected in a shift in the color predominating in their wardrobe.

Let me give you an example, one that has to do with health as it is indicated in the aura. I knew a man who from boyhood wore nothing but blue—frequently I have seen him with a blue suit, blue shirt, blue tie, and even blue socks. One day he went into a store to buy some ties. He was surprised to find that he had selected several which were maroon in color. He was even more surprised when, as time went on, he began to choose shirts with garnet stripes and ties and pocket handkerchief sets in various shades of scarlet. This went on for several years, during which time he became more nervous and more tired. He was working too hard and eventually he had a nervous breakdown.

During this time the red had grown in prominence in his aura. Now gray, the color of illness, began to creep into the red, but as he recovered, the gray disappeared and then the blue began to eat up the red. Eventually all the red was consumed and he was well. Nor did he ever afterward wear anything red, scarlet, or maroon.

In another case a woman who ordinarily wore greens and yellows, went to a dress shop which she had patronized for years. The proprietress brought out several dresses but seemed perplexed when the lady tried them on. "I don't know what it is," the proprietress said, "but you need something red or pink. I have never thought you could wear those colors, but something in you seems to call for them now." The lady eventually bought a dress with red stripes. Within a month she was in a hospital, suffering from a nervous condition. She recovered and continued to patronize the same dress shop, but the proprietress never again suggested that she wear red or pink.

Red

Red is the first of the primary colors and in ancient symbolism it represented the body, the earth, and hell, all three of which meant the same thing in the old mystery religions. The earth was the irrational world into which the soul descended from heaven. The body was the earth form which held the soul captive. Heaven was blue, and the spirit was blue. The mind was associated with yellow. It is interesting that in some systems of metaphysics blue is considered to be the true color of the sun; that is, if we could be outside earth we would see the sun as a blue light—soft, powerful and spiritual. The yellow color is supposed to result from the collision of the sun's rays with the atmosphere of earth. Since the greatest spiritual weapon of man is his intellect, it is natural that mind be associated with the sun's color in this world,

As to the meaning of red, it indicates force, vigor and energy. Its interpretation depends upon the shade, and as with all colors, upon the relationship of other colors. Dark red indicates high temper, and it is a symbol of nervous turmoil. A person with dark red in his aura may not be weak outwardly, but he is suffering in some way, and it is reflected in his nervous system. Such a person is apt to be domineering and quick to act. If the shade of red is light it indicates a nervous, impulsive, very active person, one who is probably self-centered. Scarlet indicates an overdose of ego. Pink or coral, is the color of immaturity. It is seen usually in young people, and if it shows up in the aura of one who is grown, it indicates delayed adolescence, a childish concern with self. In all cases of red, there is a tendency to nervous troubles, and such people ought to take time to be quiet and to get outside themselves.

Red is the color of the planet Mars, and corresponds to Do, the first note in the musical scale. In early Christianity it signified the suffering and death of Christ, and was the color of war, strife, and sacrifice.

Orange

Orange is the color of the sun. It is vital, and a good color generally, indicating thoughtfulness and consideration of others. Again, however, it is a matter of shade. Golden orange is vital and indicates self-control, whereas brownish orange shows a lack of ambition and a don't care attitude. Such people may be repressed, but usually they are just lazy. People with orange in their auras are subject to kidney trouble.

In the early church, orange signified glory, virtue, and the fruits of the earth, all of these being connected naturally with the sun. In the musical scales, the note Re corresponds to orange.

Yellow

Yellow is the second primary color. When it is golden yellow, it indicates health and well-being. Such people take good care of themselves, don't worry, and learn easily; good mentality is natural in them. They are happy, friendly, and helpful. If the yellow is ruddy, they are timid. If they are redheads, they are apt to have an inferiority complex. They are thus apt often to be indecisive and weak in will, inclined to let others lead them.

In the musical scale the note Mi corresponds to yellow, and Mercury is the planet of this color.

Green

Pure emerald green, particularly if it has a dash of blue, is the color of healing. It is helpful, strong, friendly. It is the color of doctors and nurses, who invariably have a lot of it in their auras. However, it is seldom a dominating color, usually being overshadowed by one of its neighbors. As it tends toward blue, it is more helpful and trustworthy. As it tends toward yellow, it is weakened. A lemony green, with a lot of yellow, is deceitful. As a rule the deep, healing green is seen in small amounts, but it is good to have a little of it in your aura.

Saturn is the planet of this color, and Fa is its musical note. In the early church, it symbolized youthfulness and the fertility of nature, taking this quite naturally from the sight of the fields in spring.

Blue

Blue has always been the color of the spirit, the symbol of contemplation, prayer, and heaven. The sky is blue because gas molecules in the air cause light rays from the sun to be scattered. This is the scientific explanation but, as I have mentioned before, blue is said to be the true color of the sun, and it is also the color of the planet Jupiter, which is the ruler of great thoughts and high-mindedness.

Almost any kind of blue is good, but the deeper shades are the best. Pale blue indicates little depth, but a struggle toward maturity. The person may not be talented, but he tries. He will have many heartaches and many headaches, but he will keep going in the right direction. The middle blue, or aqua, belongs to a person who will work harder and get more done than the fellow with light blue, though there may be little difference between them in talent. Those with the deep blue have found their work and are immersed in it. They are apt to be moody and are almost always unusual persons, but they have a mission and they steadfastly go about fulfilling it. They are spiritual-minded for the most part, and their life is usually dedicated to an unselfish cause, such as science, art, or social service. I have seen many Sisters of Mercy with this dark blue, and many writers and singers also.

The musical note of blue is Sol, and in the early church the color was assigned to the highest attainments of the soul.

Indigo and Violet

Indigo and violet indicate seekers of all types, people who are searching for a cause or a religious experience. As these people get settled in their careers and in their beliefs, however, these colors usually settle back into deep blue. It seems that once the purpose is set in the right direction, blue is a natural emanation of the soul. Those who have purple are inclined to be overbearing, for here there is an infiltration of pink. Heart trouble and stomach trouble are rather common to persons with indigo, violet, and purple in their auras.

Venus is the planet of indigo, and La is its musical note. The moon is the planet of violet and Ti is its musical note. In the early church, indigo and violet meant humiliation and sorrow.

White

The perfect color, of course, is white, and this is what we all are striving for. If our souls were in perfect balance, then all our color vibrations would blend and we would have an aura of pure white. Christ had this aura, and it is shown in many paintings of Him, particularly those which depict Him after the resurrection. You recall that He said at the tomb, "Touch me not for I am newly risen." He meant that as a warning, I think, for the vibrations of His being must at that time have been so powerful that anyone putting a hand on Him would have been killed—shocked as if by live wire.

Color is light, and light is the manifestation of creation. Without light there would be no life, and no existence. Light, in fact, is the primary witness of creation. All around us there are colors which we cannot see, just as there are sounds we cannot hear, and thoughts we cannot apprehend. Our world of comprehension is very small. We can only see the few colors between red and violet. Beyond red on one side and violet on the other are unimaginable numbers of colors, some of them so bright and wonderful, no doubt, we would be stricken blind if by some chance we could see them.

But in the fact of these colors we cannot see, these sounds we cannot hear, these thoughts we cannot apprehend, lies the hope of evolution and the promise of eternity. This is a small and narrow world, and beyond it are the glories which await our souls. But if we labor to expand our understanding and our consciousness, we can push back the limits a little bit even while here, and thus see a little more, understand a little more.

Five hundred years before the birth of Christ, Pythagoras, the first philosopher, used colors for healing. Today medical science is just beginning to see the possibilities in this method. If colors are vibrations of spiritual forces, they should be able to help in healing our deepest and most subtle maladies. Together with music, which is a kindred spiritual force, they form a great hope for therapy of the future.

But I do not think that color therapy will become widespread or practical until we have accepted the truth of auras and become accustomed to reading them in order to discover what imbalance is disturbing a person. Of course, we cannot transform all auras into a pure white light, but we can learn to detect signs of physical, mental and nervous disorders, and treat them in a proper way.

An aura is an effect, not a cause. Every atom, every molecule, every group of atoms and molecules—however simple or complex, however large or small—tells the story of itself, its pattern, its purpose, through the vibrations which emanate from it. Colors are the perceptions of these vibrations by the human eye. As the souls of individuals travel through the realms of being, they shift and change their patterns as they use or abuse the opportunities presented to them. Thus at any time, in any world, a soul will give off through vibrations the story of itself and the condition in which it now exists. If another consciousness can apprehend those vibrations, and understand them, it will know the state of its fellow being, the plight he is in, or the progress he has made.

So, when I see an aura, I see the individual as he or she is, though the details are missing. I believe the details are there, but they are missing from my perception and understanding. By experience I have learned to tell a good deal from the intensity of the colors, their distribution, and the positions they occupy. The aura emanates from the whole body, but usually it is most heavy and most easily seen around the shoulders and head, probably because of the many glandular and nervous centers located in those parts of the body. The dark shades generally denote more application, more will power, more spirit. The basic color changes as the person develops or retards, but the lighter shades and the pastels blend and shift more rapidly as the temperament expresses itself. The mind, builder of the soul, is the essential governing factor in the aura; but food, environment, and other conditions have their effect. Sometimes outside forces bring abut a change. I once met a man in whose aura I saw a shaft of light, coming downward over his left shoulder. In it there was some white, a great deal of green, and a great deal of red with blue mixed in it. I read this as a sign that the man was receiving information inspirationally, which he was using for constructive purposes. I wondered if he was a writer, for it struck me that this would be a proper aura for such work. I asked him, and he told me that although he had been a writer, he was now engaged in lecturing and teaching, still giving information for the help of others.

The shape of the aura is sometimes helpful. In children, for instance, it is possible to tell whether a great deal of training by example will be needed, or whether precept will do as well. If the child is reasonable and will accept instruction on this basis, the aura will be like a rolling crown. If example is needed, the aura will be a more definite figure, with sharp points and a variety of colors. If the child intends to be a law unto him- or herself, the aura will be like a rolling chain, lower than the position of a crown, going about the shoulders as well as the head. In the green aura of healers, if the color quivers as it rises, the person is most sympathetic. Several times I have seen people in whose auras there were little hooks of light here and there. In each case the individual had a job as overseer of large groups of others—a director and a leader.

Let me give you a few examples of aura reading. These are not complete, just some notes that were taken one day at the end of our annual Congress, when I was sitting with some of the members who had attended our meetings. Since I knew them all, I gave them only an indication of the general condition of their auras:

A woman, middle-aged: Your aura has changed more in the last three days than any I have ever seen. Your thoughts, your ideas, have wandered from the heights to the depths. At times the aura has been very beautiful, at others it has not been good. I have seen a great deal of the low, dull colors about you. Evidently something has been worrying you. It is more mental than physical.

Young woman, a secretary: There has been a great deal of red about you lately, which means that you have been rather defiant. Often I have seen lines running away from your fingers when I can't see the aura about your face. That is probably because you think with your fingers, writing so much. In the last few days you have had a great deal of purple, which means the spiritual has mingled with your defiance; your desire and hope for better things has influenced your doubts and fears. You are sure, but a little fearful at times that you will not be able to put it over. You also have a great deal of coral and pink, meaning activity, but at times you smear it with more green than white, which indicates your desire to help others irrespective of themselves. That is not God's way.

Middle-aged woman, a teacher: There is a great deal of leaden gray in your aura, not only from your physical condition, but because you have been doubting your own beliefs. You have become fearful of the thing to which you have entrusted your whole inner self. There also rise some smears of white, coming from your higher intellectual self, and from your spiritual intents and purposes. Broaden these. You also have a great deal of indigo, indicating spiritual seeking. There is green, but often fringed with red, for sometimes you would like to be in the other fellow's place, and would like him to be in your place, so that he'd know what you go through.

A middle-aged woman, social service worker: Your aura had been growing more and more to dark blue, golden, and white, with more and more white. I hope it won't entirely reach the halo, for then I would be fearful that you were leaving us. You have white with gold, which shows an ability to help others to help themselves. You have the ability to magnify the virtues of an individual, and minimize his faults.

Young woman, a clerk: Your aura is beautiful, yet often you become very fearful. At times you are easily dissatisfied. There is a great deal of blue, which is good. You should wear blue more often. You may not like it, but it will help you to think straight. You will be able to sing or hum more often as you work if you wear blue. If you don't wear it outside, wear it close to your body. There are also some minerals to which you are susceptible, particularly green stones—not because of their healing quality for you, but because of the helpful influences they will enable you to give out to others. You control others a great deal by what you say and do, more so than you realize, yet there is a great deal of coral in your aura, which means that you become fearful of your own choices and are unhappy in your environment.

Young woman, a nurse: In your aura there is a great deal of green, but you often rub it out with blue, then streak it up with red. I would not want to be around when you do the streaking, and most people who know you feel the same way, for when you let go, it is quite a display of temper. You have a good deal of ability, especially in being able to act as a healing and helpful influence to others. Consequently, the principal color in your aura is green, but you streak it up when you desire to have your own way.

Young woman, a student: Your aura is changing. There is a great deal of indigo, indicating the seeker. This indigo is not always in a regular line, but looks more like tatting all around your head. I believe this indicates that there will be a change in your relationships with certain groups of people soon.

I have given these examples to show how colors blend to form an aura, and how they change from time to time. I do not expect that many of you will be able to see these colors around others, though I am sure some of you have the power without realizing it. You can become color-conscious, and you can learn to read auras from peoples' clothes and the colors you see predominant in their surroundings—their homes, their offices, even the colors of their automobiles, their dogs, and the flowers they have selected to grow in their gardens.

It can be a fascinating game, noticing how any person with vitality and vigor will have a little splash of red in a costume, in a room, or in a garden; noticing how persons who are quiet, dependable, sure of themselves, and spiritual, never are seen without deep blues—it is almost as if they turn things blue by being near them. Notice how bright and sunny people, who like to laugh and play, and who are never tired or downhearted, will wear golden yellow and seem to color things yellow, like a buttercup held under the chin.

Colors reflect the soul and the spirit, the mind and the body, but remember they indicate lack of perfection, incompleteness. If we were all we should be, pure white would emanate from us. Strive toward that, and when you see it in others, follow it as if it were a star. It is. But we who must take solace from smaller things can draw comfort from blue, get strength from red, and be happy in the laughter and sunshine of golden yellow.

Edgar Cayce

Appendix II Examples of Edgar Cayce's Waking Aura Descriptions

Edgar Cayce Reading 288–31, Report #18:

6/21/41 Edgar Cayce's conscious reading of Miss [288]'s aura during Annual Congress meeting: "There's been a great deal of red about you lately, which means that you've been rather defiant. Very often I can see the lines running away from your fingers when I can't see the aura about your face. That's possibly because you think with your fingers, writing so much. In the last few days, though you have had a great deal of purple, which means spirituality; the desires, the hopes for better things, and yet oft shaded with doubts or fears. You are *sure*, but a little fearful at times that you're not able to 'put it over.' You also have a great deal of coral, a great deal of pink—coral *and* pink, and at times *very pink*. Then at times you smear it more with green than you do with white; which indicates your desire to help others irrespective of themselves. That's not God's way. He doesn't help one to do other than help himself. Don't forget that!"

Edgar Cayce Reading 5746-1, Report #2:
8/26/41 Gladys Davis's notes of Edgar Cayce's conscious reading of auras for those present at his Tuesday Night Bible Class—Auras read by Edgar Cayce at Tuesday Night Bible Group Meeting, August 26, 1941:

[2533]: You have more violet in your aura than anyone in the room. Violet always indicates the seeker, the searcher for something. You have more of than gray, blue, opal, white or pink. A great deal of pink or coral in an individual's aura indicates material-mindedness.

MAE ROBERTS [no case number]: You have a great deal of the shades of blue, some violet, and a little pink. So you are very definite in what you think, and in the things you do. You know where you are going, or think you know.

[641]: You have a great deal of blue, a great deal of gray—because you easily become discouraged at times. You go very much up and down; you will fly off the handle or fly on the handle just about as easy.

[1709]: You have a great deal of rose, and it becomes a very pretty aura. You judge most things by the material results that you get. I don't mean that you haven't any spirituality, but there is more of rose in your aura than the other colors. It changes, as rose would—or in coral—the changes sort of dash in and out. You smear it over, and then you streak it white and smear it over; then there's a streak of blue and you smear it over. That's the way you work.

[369]: You have a great deal of violet, pink and white. The white means purity, always. Yours runs up and down, so you are rather temperamental. Everything to you must be very definite, must be very sure, with a basis that is sound.

[1012]: You have some blue and some gray; quite a bit of purple, but your purple goes in great rolls. You have periods in which you go after a thing and you know where you are going, and then you'll have periods when you doubt whether you are going anywhere or not. Then there will come gray shadows, with rose.

[1467]: Your aura is very, very definite; it has changed since I've known you, as much as anyone I've ever seen. Your aura is a sort of crown, but in the form of long spikes that go up—and that are of varied colors. Sometimes the colors run from one shade to another; they might become very red and then very pink all along. Because you go up to the heights and then down to the depths. But you have a very good aura.

[2454]: Yours is a very beautiful aura. You could almost take it off and pin it on you and wear it, because it becomes almost like a rose that would open out and bloom, all around your head—not in rose colors, however. There is a great deal of opal, purple, and shaded along the edges with white—which makes a gold with the white and with the rose. Things are very definite with you at times, and then very uncertain at times. Then you are very sure, and you go places when you are sure.

[1223]: Your aura changes very much at times, because it goes up and down. You have a great deal of blue, but a shade of blue in the lighter shades—which would indicate your sureness as you go along with your study and your development. It opens to activities that indicate blue, white and gold. As long as you are sure you can go. When you are not sure, you stop.

[1222]: Your aura has changed a great deal in the last year or so. You have a great deal more of those colors that indicate sureness in self; orange with gold. You don't smear it, but sometimes you streak it. You get glimpses, and then you lose or miss—but your aura shows more of the seeking—with purple that usually indicates one that is seeking. Your purple goes more in clouds or rolls. There is very little of blue, which has been in your aura heretofore.

[2448]: Your aura might be called a crown entirely, with gold, purple and pink; because things must measure up materially as well as spiritually and mentally. It is very beautiful. Gold, of course, means that you have attained to some understandings in which you are very sure.

[2390]: You have a very fluffy aura, and it clouds over. There are pink and gold and purple and blue all rolled around together, and they roll over and over and over. You turn over things very systematically at times, and then you flash them through very quickly at times. You arrive very suddenly at decisions at times, then at other periods you take a long time to make up your mind. Consequently, it makes that rolling aura.

[845]: You have a light more than you have an aura. There is a light that stays about you now, which may become a part of your aura or it may be a thing that you are attaining to. But there's more of a white light that stays about you as an aura. Not many people have a white light, because when most people attain to a white light they are getting ready to do something in the way of individual accomplishment; that is, it represents that surety in which an individual has put a hope—and such an environ is created about the individual. It is not a ball of light, but more a shaft of light—that with your dark hair appears to be almost white.

[2301]: Yours is not bad! It is not unlike [2533]'s except you have a great deal of blue with your purple. Yours is not in as long spikes as [2533]'s. Consequently, in making your decisions you often make snap judgments—that is, according to your aura that would be indicated.

[404]: The last time I read your aura there were a lot of shadows about it. Now it is entirely different. I would see from your aura that you have some very unusual news coming to you. This is indicated by the way in which your aura circles about the head—a circle and one above it, and one above it; more like we usually picture a halo—a streak of gold, as that especially about a picture of the Master. There is gold and white, which would indicate good news.

[288]: This evening it has a great deal of coral, or opal coral, or a luster from it—which is very much in the form of a rolling about it; gray, white, pink, violet, all rolled into one—as if looking at a fire opal—as of a burst of enthusiasm, or burst of purpose, or individuality that would be indicated.

[2175]: Yours changes almost according to your moods. So you know about how many colors it would take. It effervesces; then you almost rub it out at times, in streaks; indicating those ideals that are your determining factors from sober thinking, and never snap judgments. When you really act on a thing you give sober judgment and thought to it. You make decisions by second thought. You flare into a thing and then you think it over. It's a mighty good thing to do, especially since there is not so much red in your aura. You don't act on things when you are mad, which is about as nice a thing as can be said about anybody. You may do something when you are mad, but you don't really mean it.

[1523]: You have a very unusual sort of aura at present. There is a great deal of gray and blue and gold. Yours is mighty high sometimes and down mighty low at other times. It is very much like a crown, but a crown with spikes—a circular crown with spikes. Violet, opal, gray, and tipped off with gold. So at times you make snap judgments, at other times you give due consideration, at other times you don't give a cuss! This is indicated by the difference in the shading of the spikes; there are two shades of red, two shades of gray, two shades of blue—in those variations.

[2378]: You have a very good aura. Most of yours is blue, with not white but a gray light. You are sometimes almost sure of yourself and then not sure at all. It doesn't take the shape of long points, or just a cloud, but more as a fold—which would be like a turban about your face and shoulders.

[1226]: You have a very unusual aura. Oftimes you smear it. There's white and gray and gold and purple. Then you smear it again. Then it may be white, purple, gold, and you smear it again. It's that sort, which would go with the assurance—and then you wonder—then you know, and then know you don't know.

[538]: Your aura has changed. It is a very nice one tonight. There is very little of pink in the aura, though most people who are material-minded have a great deal of pink. Not that you are material-minded, but you just want to be sure—and you will argue the question anyway. This is indicated in your aura, that is very much like a crown in

which there are all of the facets set above it that would be changed into the various colors of opal, blue and gold, and like that. Jewels in auras indicate definite purposes to which individuals have attained. Not very many people have them. They indicate a step in the development.

Appendix III Color Dictionary—the Possible Meaning of Colors

Note

Each individual may find her or his own subtleties in discerning the meaning of color. The following chart is provided as a potentially helpful guideline but should not supersede anyone's personal experience with the significance of a specific color.

Black May be associated with death, the unknown, and the mysterious. Might be related to evil, fear, or the end of something. Often associated with unconsciousness, negativity, or depression. Might correspond to hatred or malice, and possibly connected to black magic or the black arts.

Blue Often associated with spirituality or spiritual wisdom. Might indicate a religious or a spiritual truth. May be related to the heavenly realms or higher levels of healing.

Blue may also be associated with the following qualities: confidence, sincerity, inspiration, patience, self-reliance, trustworthiness, harmony, and artistic talent.

Significant amounts of blue in the aura may indicate that the individual is searching for her or his spiritual path and place in life. Lesser amounts of blue may indicate that the search has just begun and the individual is actively engaged in this pursuit.

Dark blue possibly indicates spiritual awakening. Pale blue may be connected with beginning the search for one's spiritual path, enhanced psychic perception, or loyalty. Blue-green might correspond to unselfish affection.

Negative expressions of blue: deep emotions that are not easily expressed, spiritual arrogance, using psychic abilities to impress others, judging the spiritual growth of others, or being too idealistic rather than realistic.

Brass May represent a false or tarnished truth. Might correspond to the fundamental ingredients of something (e.g., "the brass tacks").

Brown Often associated with that which is of the earth, as in being grounded, practical, or business-minded. Might be symbolic of materialism.

May correspond to power in the material world, or a strong work-life or ethic.

Brown may also be associated with the following qualities: being practical, favoring that which is conventional, preferring what is formal; or being organized, persistent, business-like, left-brained, logical, and impersonal.

Negative expressions of brown (especially brown/green): being selfish, a workaholic, greedy, a "stick-in-the-mud," self-serving or jealous, or having a "dog-eat-dog" mentality, judging the work of others, or neglecting or denying spiritual realities.

Coral May indicate material-mindedness (e.g., that which is beautiful but potentially dangerous). Might also be symbolic of talents or abilities that are not yet developed.

Gold Associated with spiritual truths. That which is valuable and incorruptible. May correspond to powers of the soul. Might indicate personal attainment. Often symbolizes that which is invaluable or related to the Divine. May indicate personal attainment.

Gray Often symbolic of moodiness, discouragement, or sadness. Might correspond to depression or fear. May be associated with confusion or that which is cloudy or unclear. Possibly related to the mysterious.

Gray appearing in the aura around some portion of the

body may indicate a malfunction in that area of the physical body.

Negative expressions of gray: lack of follow-through, immaturity ("Peter Pan" syndrome), empty promises, mercurial moodiness. The color gray-green may correspond to deceit. The color gray-blue might be associated with religious feelings tinged with fear.

Green Often corresponds to healing and the healing arts. May be associated with nature, growth, and development. Might be symbolic of envy (e.g., being green with envy).

Green may also be associated with the following qualities: being creative, versatile, individualistic, thoughtful, helpful, adaptable, independent, altruistic, cool and clear-headed, and being generous or loving toward others.

The color blue-green may correspond to a seeking mind, pure motives, and the desire to help mankind.

Sea green may be associated with spirituality.

A dull, murky green might indicate envy or jealousy.

Olive green might symbolize deceit, treachery, or one who is emotionally withdrawn.

Negative expressions of green: may indicate an unrealistic perfectionist or an individual who becomes overwhelmed in an emotional situation.

Indigo May be associated with a highly spiritual nature, high ideals, or spiritual wisdom. Possibly related to intuition, abundant spiritual power, and the ability to mentor others. Might be symbolic of the Christ-energy, one's higher self, or the soul.

Ivory Might indicate that something has been clouded from the truth. May relate to detachment and aloofness (e.g., "ivory tower").

Orange May be associated with creativity, personal expression, or sexuality. May be symbolic of the sun, energy, or power. Might be related to the balance of male or female energies.

Orange may also be associated with the following qualities: being energetic, vital, charming, rational, sympathetic, healthy, able to motivate others, tactful, open, and sincere. Orange in the aura might also be connected to someone destined for positions of power.

Golden-orange might be symbolic of self-control.

Brownish-orange possibly indicates apathy or a lack of personal ambition.

Negative expressions of orange (especially dull, reddish orange): may indicate selfishness, pride, being easily influenced or emotionally hurt by others, having trouble balancing the mental or head with the emotional or heart, and being prone to wavering.

Pink May indicate the influence of love and affection. Possibly associated with divine love or physical health (e.g., "in the pink"). Might symbolize youth or immaturity.

Purple May correspond to high-mindedness, high mental abilities, or higher vibrations. Possibly associated with spiritual healing. Might be symbolic of royalty (or a royal past life), or loyalty.

Purple may also be associated with spiritual development, wisdom, initiation, or mastery of self through life's experiences.

Red Associated with energy, force, passion, and vigor. May be indicative of rage, aggressiveness, a temper, or anger. Might be symbolic of danger or represent the color of blood.

Red may also be associated with the following qualities: strength, vitality, having a generous nature, strong-mindedness, courage, possessing a commanding nature, having a magnetic personality, or being strong-willed or defiant.

Negative expressions of red: Cloudy red or dull-brown red may correspond to greed or a materialistic outlook. Dark red may be symbolic of a tendency toward selfishness, revenge, hatred, violence, or cruelty. Crimson red might correspond to a propensity to sensuality or lust.

Rose Associated with beauty, love, and the manifestation of nature. Light rose may correspond to a love for humanity.

Silver May correspond to that which is of material value. Might be associated with higher levels of consciousness. Often seen in the very young or immature personalities as "flashes," rather than as a dominant color.

Silver may also be associated with the following qualities: being versatile, charming, a jack-of-all-trades, active, lively, or possessing the "gift of gab."

Negative expressions of silver (especially silver-gray): May correspond to someone who is living as a loner, experiencing depression, or exhibiting poor health.

Violet Associated with great spirituality or spiritual attainment. May correspond to a connection to the Divine or oneness. May indicate higher states of consciousness or spiritual healing.

Violet may also be associated with the following qualities: attaining spiritual power, influence, or spiritual greatness, being a seeker, or possessing true idealism or altruistic love.

Violet is rarely seen in the aura. It contains the spirituality of blue and the red of vitality and power. It is often the color of the spiritual initiate or the spiritually adept.

White Important note: generally, those who begin working with auras will see "white" surrounding the aura. It might be seen as a haze, a smoke, or a cloud. At this point in the intuitive process, the eyes have yet to be able to differentiate the variations of color. Later on and with practice, when seeing white, the regular color definition may be more appropriate.

White may be indicative of purity, innocence, holiness, and perfection. The white light is associated with the Divine. It may correspond to wholeness, balance, and the complete integration of all colors of the spectrum. It may also be associated with selfless service. It is symbolic of the ultimate ideal.

Yellow Often associated with thoughts and ideas. Might correlate to energy, personal power, and self-confidence.

Yellow may also be associated with the following qualities: intelligence, excellent concentration, optimism, business acumen, the ability to stimulate the health and mind of others, the ability to dispel fear and worry in others, and possessing an outstanding teaching ability.

Pale yellow may correspond to one who is high-spirited, thoughtful, perceptive, developing spiritual qualities, and able to get things done rather than just thinking about them.

Negative expressions of yellow (especially dark, dingy yellow): being suspicious, impractical, thoughtless, or being a dreamer, e.g., thinking about doing things but never starting.

References and Recommended Reading

Cayce, Edgar. *Auras: An Essay on the Meaning of Colors.* Virginia Beach, Virginia: A.R.E. Press, 1945.

Kilner, Walter J. *The Human Aura.* New Hyde Park, New York: University Books, 1965.

Lewis, Roger. *Color and the Edgar Cayce Readings.* Virginia Beach, Virginia: A.R.E. Press, 1973.

Liaros, Carol Ann. *Aura Scan.* Creative Community Institute: Amherst, New York: no date. Audiocassette.

Liaros, Carol Ann. *Intuition Made Easy.* Scottsdale, Arizona: Cloudbank Creations, Inc., 2003.

Ostrander, Sheila, Nancy Ostrander, and Lynn Schroeder. *Super-Learning.* New York, New York: Dell Publishing Company, 1979.

Puryear PhD, Herbert B. and Mark A. Thurston, PhD. *Meditation and the Mind of Man.* Virginia Beach, Virginia: A.R.E. Press, 1983.

Todeschi, Kevin J. *Dream Images and Symbols: A Dictionary.* Virginia Beach, Virginia: A.R.E. Press, 2003.

Todeschi, Kevin J. *Edgar Cayce on Vibrations.* Virginia Beach, Virginia: A.R.E. Press, 2007.

Todeschi, Kevin J. *Soul Signs: Life Seals, Aura Charts, and the Revelation.* Virginia Beach, Virginia: A.R.E. Press, 2003.

Tutko, Agatha P., "Teaching the Blind to See," *Fate Magazine*, May 1975.

About the Authors

KEVIN J. TODESCHI is the Executive Director and CEO of Edgar Cayce's Association for Research and Enlightenment, overseeing activities of the Cayce work worldwide. As both student and teacher of the Edgar Cayce material for more than thirty years, he has lectured on five continents in front of thousands of individuals. A prolific writer, he is the author of more than twenty books, including *Edgar Cayce on the Akashic Records, Edgar Cayce on Soul Mates,* and *Edgar Cayce on Reincarnation and Family Karma.*

CAROL ANN LIAROS has been a professional psychic for over forty years. In addition to working with Edgar Cayce's A.R.E. for more than twenty-five years, she has worked with business leaders and corporate executives, psychotherapists, health organizations, churches, and spiritual groups. As the subject of psychic research with E. Douglas Dean, PhD, Sister M. Justa Smith, PhD, and Shafica Karagulla, M.D., her accuracy over a two-year study was 93–97 percent in predicting the future. A very popular workshop leader and presenter, she is also the author of *Intuition Made Easy.*

A.R.E. Press

Edgar Cayce (1877–1945) founded the non-profit Association for Research and Enlightenment (A.R.E.) in 1931, to explore spirituality, holistic health, intuition, dream interpretation, psychic development, reincarnation, and ancient mysteries—all subjects that frequently came up in the more than 14,000 documented psychic readings given by Cayce.

Edgar Cayce's A.R.E. provides individuals from all walks of life and a variety of religious backgrounds with tools for personal transformation and healing at all levels—body, mind, and spirit.

A.R.E. Press has been publishing since 1931 as well, with the mission of furthering the work of A.R.E. by publishing books, DVDs, and CDs to support the organization's goal of helping people to change their lives for the better physically, mentally, and spiritually.

In 2009, A.R.E. Press launched its second imprint, 4th Dimension Press. While A.R.E. Press features topics directly related to the work of Edgar Cayce and often includes excerpts from the Cayce readings, 4th Dimension Press allows us to take our publishing efforts further with like-minded and expansive explorations into the mysteries and spirituality of our existence without direct reference to Cayce specific content.

Edgar Cayce's A.R.E.

Who Was Edgar Cayce?
Twentieth Century Psychic and Medical Clairvoyant

Edgar Cayce (pronounced Kay-Cee, 1877-1945) has been called the "sleeping prophet," the "father of holistic medicine," and the most-documented psychic of the 20th century. For more than 40 years of his adult life, Cayce gave psychic "readings" to thousands of seekers while in an unconscious state, diagnosing illnesses and revealing lives lived in the past and prophecies yet to come. But who, exactly, was Edgar Cayce?

Cayce was born on a farm in Hopkinsville, Kentucky, in 1877, and his psychic abilities began to appear as early as his childhood. He was able to see and talk to his late grandfather's spirit, and often played with "imaginary friends" whom he said were spirits on the other side. He also displayed an uncanny ability to memorize the pages of a book simply by sleeping on it. These gifts labeled the young Cayce as strange, but all Cayce really wanted was to help others, especially children.

Later in life, Cayce would find that he had the ability to put himself into a sleep-like state by lying down on a couch, closing his eyes, and folding his hands over his stomach. In this state of relaxation and meditation, he was able to place his mind in contact with all time and space—the universal consciousness, also known as the super-conscious mind. From there, he could respond to questions as broad as, "What are the secrets of the universe?" and "What is my purpose in life?" to as specific as, "What can I do to help my arthritis?" and "How were the pyramids of Egypt built?" His responses to these questions came to be called "readings," and their insights offer practical help and advice to individuals even today.

The majority of Edgar Cayce's readings deal with holistic health and the treatment of illness. Yet, although best known for this material, the sleeping Cayce did not seem to be limited to concerns about the physical body. In fact, in their entirety, the readings discuss an astonishing 10,000 different topics. This vast array of subject matter can be narrowed down into a smaller group of topics that, when compiled together, deal with the following five categories: (1) Health-Related Information; (2) Philosophy and Reincarnation; (3) Dreams and Dream Interpretation; (4) ESP and Psychic Phenomena; and (5) Spiritual Growth, Meditation, and Prayer.

Learn more at EdgarCayce.org.

What Is A.R.E.?

Edgar Cayce founded the non-profit Association for Research and Enlightenment (A.R.E.) in 1931, to explore spirituality, holistic health, intuition, dream interpretation, psychic development, reincarnation, and ancient mysteries—all subjects that frequently came up in the more than 14,000 documented psychic readings given by Cayce.

The Mission of the A.R.E. is to help people transform their lives for the better, through research, education, and application of core concepts found in the Edgar Cayce readings and kindred materials that seek to manifest the love of God and all people and promote the purposefulness of life, the oneness of God, the spiritual nature of humankind, and the connection of body, mind, and spirit.

With an international headquarters in Virginia Beach, Va., a regional headquarters in Houston, regional representatives throughout the U.S., Edgar Cayce Centers in more than thirty countries, and individual members in more than seventy countries, the A.R.E. community is a global network of individuals.

A.R.E. conferences, international tours, camps for children and adults, regional activities, and study groups allow like-minded people to gather for educational and fellowship opportunities worldwide.

A.R.E. offers membership benefits and services that include a quarterly body-mind-spirit member magazine, *Venture Inward*, a member newsletter covering the major topics of the readings, and access to the entire set of readings in an exclusive online database.

Learn more at EdgarCayce.org.

EDGARCAYCE.ORG